BENJAMIN FRANKLIN'S

THE WAY TO WEALTH

BENJAMIN FRANKLIN'S
THE WAY TO WEALTH

A 52 BRILLIANT IDEAS INTERPRETATION
BY STEVE SHIPSIDE

First published in 2008 by
Infinite Ideas Limited
36 St Giles
Oxford
OX1 3LD
United Kingdom
www.infideas.com

A CIP catalogue record for this book is available from the British Library

ISBN 978–1–904902–84–3

Designed and typeset by Cylinder
Printed in India

BRILLIANT IDEAS

 INTRODUCTION

Turning the pages of Benjamin Franklin's *The Way to Wealth* is a bit like going into the attic of your parents' house and sifting through all the old family belongings. There are so many aphorisms and bite-sized bits of homely wisdom that you begin to wonder if this was what your granny read before going to bed every night of her life. 'Early to bed and early to rise…', 'no gains without pains', 'little strokes fell great oaks', 'God helps those that helps themselves' – it's as if every drop of sound and solemn common sense you ever heard had been distilled into the pages of one slim volume. As a true classic it's also clear, on reflection, that this advice is as valid now as it was back in 1758 when the book was published. Creditors still make killings off unwary borrowers and working smarter, not harder, is still the way to business success. So why would you read a modern interpretation of an already stick-thin tract? Two reasons, really. The first is that, like everything else in the attic, *The Way to Wealth* has picked up a little bit of dust on the way. Groats and grindstones generally play little part in our daily lives these days. Similarly work tends to revolve around management, delivering services, knowledge work rather than 'spinning and knitting… hewing and splitting'. Apologies if any senior hewing and splitting executives out there feel slighted by this. More importantly, Franklin was writing in an era when manual labour and the delivery of products rather than services were the primary activities. As such he doesn't dwell much on knowledge management, outsourcing or even delegation. What is surprising, then, is how much of his homespun wisdom still applies to those fields (with a little extrapolation).

But most of all the problem posed by *The Way to Wealth* is that it is, as Franklin himself puts it, a 'harangue'. It's told as a tale within a tale, with the advice within being delivered as a sermon by a fiercely anti-materialistic disciplinarian called Father Abraham. In the book the narrator is a writer called Richard Saunders who recognises that Abraham's words are in fact his own advice (or as he acknowledges, the collected advice of generations) being read back to him.

By making himself a character in the text, and having that character be lectured, Franklin makes it clear he is aware that so much good advice delivered in one chunk is like having your ear bent. By your grandparents. Which is never that comfortable and leaves me, for one, with the uneasy feeling that I'm being told how to invest money that I had previously earmarked for gobstoppers and sherbet dip dabs.

That tone alone is enough to have modern adults quietly putting the book down after only a few lines. Which is a pity because Franklin reserves a little surprise at the end which explains why he has the advice delivered by the daunting Father Abraham rather than by himself. Despite being written as a harangue, *The Way to Wealth* is a very human book about very human strengths and weaknesses. If this modernisation helps keep alive even a small part of that homely wisdom in the context of today's high-tech world then Franklin would have approved. Only he wouldn't have put it that way, of course. He'd probably have nodded sagely and muttered something along the lines of 'many a little makes a mickle'. And how right he'd have been.

1 USE IT OR LOSE IT

As Franklin puts it, *'sloth, like rust, consumes faster than labor wears, while the used key is always bright.'* These days we'd most likely skip the key/rust analogy and simply say 'use it or lose it'.

Franklin was literally an expert on the potential of used keys, having once attached one to a kite and flown it into a thunderstorm as part of an experiment into electricity. Indeed, as a physicist and inventor – as well as a musician, writer and politician – you could say he was an expert on energy of all kinds.

DEFINING IDEA...

Cultivate all your faculties; you must either use them or lose them.
~ JOHN LUBBOCK, ENGLISH BIOLOGIST AND POLITICIAN

The idea that the brain can be exercised and even trained to perform better is one that has long fascinated scientists and continues to be a source of heated debate today. What we know for sure is that learning is partly a function of brain cells making connections with each other as they fire, so that as we repeat a task and those cells fire repeatedly they wire together a bit like an electronics circuit. When you repeat an activity, that circuit kicks in and performs better and faster than your initial attempts. It has also been observed that different parts of the brain can be retrained. For example, the visual cortex doesn't cease to function in blind people just because there is no visual information to process; indeed there is evidence that it is active in interpreting Braille. So the argument goes that the brain can be trained like a muscle to get stronger and stay stronger for longer.

Medical studies into brain training have mainly focused on older adults (the group most concerned with losing brain power) and have shown that these older adults will show improvements in memory and attention when they are given thinking games and tasks.

In Japan the concept of brain training has taken off and become a major industry with the Nintendo game *Dr Kawashima's Brain Training: How Old is Your Brain?* selling millions of copies in the Japanese market alone in its first year. The idea is that you play a series of daily tasks involving logic and maths and are rated with a 'brain age' to see how your brain gets 'younger' depending on the mental agility you show as you become better and faster at the games. The brand has since been exported, as well as widely imitated, and brain-training games are now available as console games, mobile phone applications or even good old-fashioned books.

There are just a couple of provisos, though. The first is that with all the emphasis on older adults there isn't so much data on benefits for young people and the second is that, as with any specific learning task, you're not training the brain to be a more intelligent brain – just one that's better at completing the tasks it's being set. Which leads some to wonder whether the goal of their grey matter is to leap over the hurdles Dr Kawashima chooses to set in its path.

HERE'S AN IDEA FOR YOU...

You don't need to buy a Nintendo or indeed any branded brain games to give your grey matter a good going over. A lot of 'brain games' are simply variations on classics like crosswords and Sudoku, so give those a try. Many scientists think that stimulation is the real key.

2 BE THE DRIVER, NOT THE DRONE

Despite an overwhelming emphasis on hard work and honest labour Franklin is very clear about the importance of keeping control of your work life. Or, as he puts it, *'drive thy business, let not that it drive thee.'*

As a man who packed half a dozen careers into his life, Franklin well understood the need to manage his tasks so that he remained in control of his work, rather than the other way around.

DEFINING IDEA…

The way we measure productivity is flawed. People checking their BlackBerry over dinner is not the measure of productivity.

~ TIMOTHY FERRISS,
AUTHOR OF THE 4-HOUR WORK WEEK

Go to different parts of the world and you will find some dramatically different work cultures at play. I once worked for an American technology company who were simultaneously setting up offices in the UK, Germany and France. The New Yorker overseeing this launch based himself mainly in London where he found that his new employees might speak with strange accents but at least he could understand the way they worked; they rapidly adopted his pattern of staying at work until deep into the night and understanding that 'lunch' meant a hurriedly-snatched sandwich eaten at the keyboard. The Germans and the French, on the other hand… Well, the French insisted fiercely that lunch was not an intake of calories but rather a venue you went to, and by 5 p.m. the German office only needed a bit of tumbleweed blowing through to be the model for a Wild West ghost town. But neither was any less productive. The French did much of their most important negotiation over lunch and the German approach was that anyone still in the office after 5 p.m. was clearly a poor time manager who couldn't do their job properly.

In the US there is now a backlash against the idea that a good worker is one who spends all their time in front of their keyboard. One of the bestselling books is *The 4-Hour Work Week* by Timothy Ferriss who realised that his work life in Silicon Valley was unsustainable after his girlfriend left him over his work hours. We can learn from his mistake without sacrificing our love lives.

One of Ferriss's rules, for instance, is that he only checks his email once a week. That may sound extreme but his point is that because he only replies on a set day, his customers and co-workers have adapted and his business doesn't fall apart. And he spends a fraction of his time dealing with email.

So remember Franklin and don't let your business run your life. Stop seeing time spent at work (yours or your employees') as being automatically good, and start thinking about whether those long hours mean productivity or a failure to empower people. We all know that it's easier to waste time in front of a computer so take a leaf from the Germans and encourage a culture where long hours, far from being approved of, are instead frowned on as a sure sign of poor time management.

HERE'S AN IDEA FOR YOU...

Set aside a strict time slot in the morning (or morning and evening, if you must) and don't even look at your email outside of that. Let others know this is your routine and you'll be surprised how much less time you spend digging your way out of an inbox.

3 PLAY THE TIME ZONE GAME

'Early to bed, and early to rise, makes a man healthy, wealthy and wise.' Fine words, and ones you've probably heard not just from Franklin but from any number of slightly smug older relatives and colleagues.

Yes, it's good advice, but here's a modern twist to it. In this day and age, who says that you are the one who has to get up early?

DEFINING IDEA...

Early morning hath gold in its mouth.

~ BENJAMIN FRANKLIN

In the mid-90s the World Wide Web was just finding its feet and sharper businesses were working out how to use it in order to steal a march on their competition. One of the earliest stories to surface and raise eyebrows was the news that some American medical doctors, rather than typing up their notes themselves, were instead taking digital dictation and sending it over the Net to India where it was transcribed overnight and emailed back, all ready, for the start of the next working day. People have long dreamed of waking up to find their work done for them but, given the general shortage of shoemaker's elves in today's world, that prospect seemed destined to remain a dream. And then suddenly the ability to export work at the touch of a button made businesses aware that they could not only outsource to save money, but to play the time zone game and steal a day in the process.

Outsourcing has acquired a bit of a bad name in the interim, with associations of job losses and service levels being sacrificed for the sake of cost, but while bad news travels fast and loudly the good news tends to be kept as a trade secret. So it is that knowledge of call centre calamities has become common currency but you rarely hear about the software development teams handing over their work every night to their waking colleagues on the other side of the globe.

Nor is it just multinational corporations who can exploit time zone differences, and you don't have to hire a truck-load of typists in Trincomalee to get the benefit of other people working around the clock for you. In these days of remote and virtual working, it is even sometimes cost-effective to outsource just an hour or two of work in a day to somebody else, and there is a growing number of flexible workers (often retired people or perhaps downshifters) who can be extremely useful – they are highly qualified, time-rich and interested in taking on piece work at a competitive price. If you have to do something like make routine calls or catch up on your admin at unsociable hours, why not have these sort of comparatively straightforward tasks fielded by outsourced early birds? Particularly if those early birds have chosen to relocate eastwards on retirement and have an hour or two advance on you in any case? Think about that the next time you wake up and swear at your alarm clock.

HERE'S AN IDEA FOR YOU...

Tim Ferriss, author of The 4-Hour Work Week, points out that almost anyone can outsource and even claims to outsource his personal to-do lists and email inbox to a virtual PA in India who organises his life while he sleeps. Do some investigating for yourself.

4 NO PAIN, NO GAIN

And you thought that saying was invented in the age of lycra, right? As it happens Benjamin Franklin beat Jane Fonda to it by a couple of hundred years when he pointed out that *'there are no gains, without pains'*.

While Franklin's reaction to spandex-sheathed aerobicisers can only be imagined, the association of 'no pain, no gain' with exercise has at least helped clarify his point for a modern audience. You might personally jeer at joggers but you're almost certainly familiar with the idea that out of suffering comes a better body, increased fitness and decreased blubber.

What you may not be doing, however, is applying that same understanding to business. The fitness freak knows that it's not going to be easy and so accepts, even welcomes, the discomfort and short-term agony of working for the burn. In business, however, we're often so focused on breathless expansion that we fail to prepare for the pain that will inevitably come as part of the package.

When planning on expansion or change, businesspeople often focus solely on more obvious pains such as increased outgoings and management overheads. More easily overlooked are the personal and cultural pains that accompany almost every business gain, which is where our gym bunnies are so helpful. They focus on the gain and accept the pain as the only means of getting there. Business, on the other hand, often forgets to do so. Here's an example of what I mean. I can remember when computers made their appearance in business and, as a journalist, I was one of many encouraged to switch over to them. The journalists' union was up in arms, proposing extra payment for being forced to use this new and daunting technology and leading to a classic management/union stand-off. Nobody attempted to go to the journalists and explain that the real gain was our own individual productivity and employability in the future. Everyone got caught up over whether we should be paid for the sweat; nobody extolled the beauty of the svelte and desirable souls we would become (I'm talking figuratively here – if you've ever seen an office full of journalists you'll know that).

You don't have to have a large unionised workforce to run into cultural resistance to expansion. Resistance to change usually comes in one of two forms – active and passive. It's normal to see active resisters as being the enemy. They're not. Your real problem is the passive resisters who mentally fold their arms and say 'make me'. Small enterprises are just as susceptible as larger ones, too, though often more subtly so. The classic person to overlook is yourself and your own resistance. With growth comes the need to delegate more and micromanage less, so you may feel a sense of losing your grip on your own company. Fail to deal with that pain and you will never realise the gain, which is one of the key factors why so many sole traders and family businesses never grow any further.

HERE'S AN IDEA FOR YOU...

Don't stand up and tell people they have to change or it will become personal. Instead start by explaining that the change is best practice learnt from others and find the people most open to that idea. Now make them change stewards/agents and recruit their help instead of going it alone.

5 SO ARE YOU FEELING LUCKY?

'Diligence is the mother of good luck,' said Franklin. Gary Player, the extraordinary golfer, put it differently. He was once told he was a 'lucky' player. 'Yes,' he replied, 'and the more I practise the luckier I get.'

DEFINING IDEA...

What we call luck is the inner man externalised. We make things happen to us.

~ ROBERTSON DAVIES,
CANADIAN WRITER AND NOVELIST

There will always be an element of luck when it comes to human affairs, and business is no exception. That chance meeting that leads to a contract, the stumbling across a new idea, or partner, or supplier – you can call it serendipity, or you can call it plain jammy, but whatever you call it we all think that luck has its part to play. The difference is that the seriously successful believe that luck is something you make by working at it.

The simple soul turns up for a meeting or a deal with the belief that their knowledge of their own company and goals, plus their individual bargaining skills, should be enough to tip the balance in their direction. The more savvy individuals dig a bit further to make some luck by researching the other party, the market, the people involved, the other company's culture, the other company's national culture and absolutely anything else that they think could have a bearing on the hidden agenda or the triggers to behaviour. If they then stumble on a shared interest with the other party, one that smoothes the way to an agreement, do you call that luck or good research?

In this day and age, with the availability of search engines, online newspaper archives (both local and national) and social software such as LinkedIn, there is no excuse for not putting in that little bit of extra effort to find out more about someone. You don't have to be a sad cyberstalker to get the information you need. If your opposite number has a Facebook page which includes a mention of Accrington Stanley Football Club, for instance, you can be fairly sure that they are a fan and will be happy to meet anyone who shares their interest (especially so if they are one of a rare breed such as Accrington Stanley supporters). So do some research into that, too. Find out more before you begin, and then practise how you will turn that to your advantage.

There will always be naturals, it is true, but for every natural there is a natural-seeming businessperson who has ruthlessly rehearsed their social skills, knowledge and delivery until their whole performance is so slick that it seems perfectly spontaneous – not at all like a performance, in fact. A delivery so practised that it passes for one that is completely natural can get you through any number of situations. As the French playwright Jean Giraudoux once put it '…the secret of success is sincerity. Once you can fake that you've got it made'.

HERE'S AN IDEA FOR YOU…

Think first impressions. Salesmen know about the 'elevator pitch' where you lay out your key attributes and goal in three minutes. You should be able to do this. Sit down in front of a mirror with a stopwatch and see how good you sound in that time. Would you recommend you to someone else?

6 SLUGS, SPEEDSTERS AND DEAD SHARKS

'Laziness travels so slowly,' observed Franklin, 'that poverty soon overtakes him.' The obvious modern interpretation of this is that anyone who takes their foot off the pedal and slacks off is eventually going to find financial worries snapping at their heels.

Fair enough, and as true today as it was back in 1758, but the march of time has added another dimension to Franklin's wisdom. Woody Allen famously declared that 'A relationship, I think, is like a shark, you know? It has to constantly move forward or it dies. And I think what we got on our hands is a dead shark.' Replace the word 'relationship' with the word 'business'…

Physical laziness is easy to recognise, but intellectual laziness tends to be harder to spot and much easier to disguise with rationalisations. With the rapid pace and constant evolution of today's business landscape, simply working hard is not enough to guarantee success. The truly successful are also constantly scanning the horizon for new opportunities and threats.

Established back in 1873, Barnes and Noble was the giant of the American bookselling industry with over 800 shops by the 1990s. The company could quite reasonably claim to be the barons of bookselling. But a quick-witted entrepreneur called Jeff Bezos had already latched on to the potential that this new-fangled World Wide Web thingy offered for remote sales, and while he professed no knowledge of the book trade he chose books as a good starting point for a new company selling online. The result was that the barons of bookselling suddenly found themselves under attack from an unexpected upstart. The 'Amazon effect', in which a new competitor appears out of nowhere thanks to technology, has since kept CEOs awake at night all over the globe.

The point is that if you're not evolving your business then you are surely killing it off. Here's an example. A smart business keeps abreast of developments in its own market sector. A really smart business looks beyond its own trade or market and follows trends in other, seemingly unconnected, areas with a view to poaching good ideas or practices that can give them that crucial boost. You don't have to work in the clothing business, for instance, to learn lessons from Marks and Spencer's automated supply line – items sold at the till automatically trigger an order to restock right down the line to the suppliers themselves.

A few hundred years ago a successful business model would be good for a generation, and, with a bit of tweaking from your children, might see that business carry on for another generation. Now standing still means you wind up with a big dead fish on your hands. Your business isn't healthy if you're not already working on how to take it to the next level.

HERE'S AN IDEA FOR YOU...

You can begin to look beyond your own business area for learning opportunities quite easily. Get hold of the trade magazines from a completely different industry and see how they are innovating in the management of people, products, processes and services.

7 DEBT AND DESPAIR

If Franklin was around today he'd be on Oprah. *'Industry pays debts, while despair increaseth them'* was his advice. It's a pity that so many of us fail to heed it.

Debt, drug dependency and depression are pretty much the grim horsemen of the modern apocalypse, intertwined and mutually provocative as they are. What Franklin was pointing out all those years ago wasn't just that hard work pays debts, but that frozen immobility actually fuels them. What's often forgotten is the painful truth that throwing yourself into work may not be enough to dig your way out of the hole and could even just contribute to the problem.

DEFINING IDEA…

He who promises runs in debt.

~ THE TALMUD

In the animal kingdom there are countless examples of small beasties that freeze to avoid the attentions of larger, hungrier ones. Fair play, and if it wasn't a successful strategy then there wouldn't be so many beasties still around pretending not to be there. The catch is that while this will probably save you repeatedly from peckish predators, it does precisely diddley squat for your chances when it comes to avoiding the dinosaur that is about to stomp on you simply because you're in its path. Debt is that vast, short-sighted diplodocus plodding your way. It doesn't matter whether you act the stick insect and freeze, or the ant and toil all the more furiously because that's how you've always dealt with life. Either way, the arrival of the overgrown lizard is going to leave you equally flat.

So deal with the debt dinosaur before the debt dinosaur deals with you. Debt happens; indeed it is a normal part of life for all but a rare few. Whether we're talking personal finances or company balance sheets, the problems occur when debt grows beyond our ability to manage it. And this is the point at which it quickly transforms into the scaly, unavoidable behemoth.

The first thing to do is to recognise it and stop pretending it's not there. If there is a quick-fix means of cutting your debt down to size then do it immediately – whether that means chopping up your credit card and transferring the balance or reining in the executive expenses. The chances are that by the time you recognise the problem the quick fixes will only buy you time and won't be enough to clear the backlog. The next step is to talk to your creditors. This will not be easy especially as the natural instinct, whether personal or corporate, is to put doing it off. So make a virtue of a sticky situation and be as open and transparent as possible. You're not going to look good for getting into debt, but any creditor who suspects that you are hiding even more debt is going to lose faith in you altogether. This is as true for banks as it is for anyone – trading partners, foreign governments and maiden aunts.

Coming clean is the first step towards coming up with solutions.

HERE'S AN IDEA FOR YOU...

Talk to someone; Oprah and Franklin would be united about this. Your debt isn't unique. Sharing the load will go a long way to dealing with the despair, making it easier to shift into action and deal with it. The first, and hardest, step is to stop the denial and address the problem.

8 TO THINE OWN SELF BE TRUE

'The second vice is lying, the first is running in debt,' says Franklin, implying that while honest people can run into debt, the act of being in debt may make them lie about it.

DEFINING IDEA...

Oh what a wicked web we weave, when first we practice to deceive.

~ SIR WALTER SCOTT

Which comes first? Debt or denial? According to Franklin it is failing to keep your finances on the straight and narrow that leads to falsehood and from there to the slippery slope. Which is true, but not necessarily in the way you're thinking. It's not that everyone in debt lies to others, but that the vast majority of those in debt lie to themselves. Don't believe it? Try a simple question: how much do you owe?

A debt audit is rarely as clear cut as you think because everyone in debt rationalises their situation by mentally rebranding debt as something else. It's a remarkably efficient technique – just consider how much less attractive a credit card would sound if it was called, more accurately, a debt card.

So let's start with credit cards. Do you really know how much you owe, exactly, on your cards this month? Are you completely sure you know how many cards you have that debt spread over? Nor is it enough to be able to glibly reel off the precise figure – in order to really know how much debt you have, you also have to know the current interest rate your card is charging you because that will affect how much you owe. A fair few of us might be able to say with some certainty how much they owe, but few of us could give the rate exactly, not least since it has undoubtedly changed since you took out the card.

Now what about the mortgage? I know, it seems churlish to consider the mortgage as a debt since almost everyone has got one and it's undoubtedly the most socially acceptable form of debt. But it is a debt, nonetheless, with a monthly repayment of which – again – you should know the exact rate.

Any other loans? Cars? Consolidation loans? Overdraft? Home improvement? OK, toss them into the pile. Now the nasty ones. Store cards? Go and find out the interest rate; chances are, you're in for a very unpleasant shock.

Finally, don't forget that anything you don't pay for until after you've used it is effectively a loan, even if it's (initially) an interest-free one. If you have a pay as you go phone then it's fine, but if you're on a contract then you're already running up a bill you haven't yet been asked to pay.

When you take into account everything you really owe, you'll probably find it a bit of a shock. Personally, when forced to look at my total debts, I find it best to do so from behind the relative safety of the sofa. Scary? You betcha, but not as bad as pretending that the debt's not there and will go away by itself.

HERE'S AN IDEA FOR YOU...

Some debt can be balanced at less cost; take a look at the interest rates you're paying. Start with the store cards, they're probably the worst. If you can't pay them off with cash (the optimum solution), consider using an overdraft – a much cheaper way of borrowing. Then shred them.

9 CONDUCT YOUR OWN ANNUAL REVIEW

'If you were a servant, would you not be ashamed that a good master should catch you idle?' notes Franklin, before concluding then that *'are you then your own master, be ashamed to catch yourself idle.'* So, as your own master, how do you think you're getting on?

DEFINING IDEA...

What is interesting about self-analysis is that it leads nowhere – it is an art form in itself.

~ ANITA BROOKNER

Whether you are employed or self-employed, take a moment out to assess yourself. Be realistic and honestly rate how well you're doing. Now, like so many people I set up my own business mainly because I loved the idea of being my own boss. But, also like so many others, I suspect that if I were honest with myself, I would admit to being a lousy boss with a notable inability to clamp down on day-long lunch breaks. Hmm – see what I mean?

Time to get stuck in. Be as objective as you can. Now, as with any annual review, this shouldn't just be about putting a person (OK, you) on the spot and asking them what they think they could do better. Instead it should be part of a process aimed at encouraging you to think more about what you've achieved and what you could go on to achieve. As such, it should be accompanied by an annual audit of exactly what you have done, and a brain-dump of goals to be set for the next year. At the risk of developing schizophrenia, this is quite a good moment to stand on both sides of the divide and see your goals and achievements both as your employer and as your employee.

As your employer, do you feel that the last year's workload, targets and ambition were completely satisfactory? As the employee, do you feel that your employer is perhaps being over-optimistic, given the undoubted demands on your time?

Remember that the more you break down the achievements and/or goals into their component skills and stages the clearer an idea you will have of exactly where you are shooting wide. Don't just tick the box and say 'yup, I did fine' but try to think about where you did well in achieving something, where you could have done better, and who else had valuable input from which you could learn something useful.

Any good review is not simply about appraising degrees of success but about actually learning from them and plotting a path to improvement. The result of your assessment should therefore be a plan for moving on from past problems. The first step of that, as with so many ten-step plans, is admitting that you do indeed have failings. A self-assessment is strictly hush-hush, so this is one of the few opportunities to really be honest with yourself. And if you genuinely don't think you have any failings then you can put 'lack of self-awareness' right slap at the top of your list.

HERE'S AN IDEA FOR YOU...

Review your job description. Most self-employed people don't really have one, so if you're self-employed think about what your title would be if you were part of a larger company. Is that where you want to be? This is a great way of focusing on what you really do.

10 DON'T MICROMANAGE

Franklin is often misunderstood on this point since he is adamant that you should do your own work and not rely on others to do it for you. There is one key proviso he adds to that, namely that *'the eye of a master will do more work than both his hands'*…

DEFINING IDEA...

Micromanaging is ridiculous. There's always a certain amount of dynamic tension, which is good because it stimulates creative thinking. But what we want to look for is a balance where each body or group of people is fulfilling their role.

~ KARIN UHLICH, POLITICIAN

Now, this is a particular problem for those who have started their own businesses or who have come up through the ranks of a business, getting their hands suitably dirty on the way. It's an old truism of many industries that the way they reward good workers is to promote them away from what they did well in the first place, thereby leaving that work to be done by less able colleagues instead. What's often forgotten is that there is a flip side to that truism, which is that the more able workers are often reluctant to let go of their hands-on skill and are resistant to the new role that they have to play. Translating hands-on experience into the ability to train, manage or assess the work of others is not necessarily the smooth transition we all have the tendency to assume it will be.

Micromanaging doesn't just mean that you try and do everything yourself; it can also mean that you don't allow others the free rein to come up with their own solutions or style. Which doesn't mean that you know best – just that you're not listening. If you're tempted to describe your workers as blockheads it could be that you have blockheads working for you (you wouldn't be the first, of course) or it could be that your style of management has so taken the initiative away from your workers that they see no real incentive for trying to sort out problems for themselves. Like a bad workman blaming his tools, the hard-core micromanager curses the dumbness of his staff while silencing them with his work style. Or her work style, of course.

You might think you have to be a raging psychopath to be a micromanager, but you don't. The chances are that you're just hanging on to a way of doing things that you liked when you were the one doing it and are resisting the idea that those times and ways have gone, probably for ever. The problem, indeed the likelihood, is that in the process you may be discouraging any development from the major asset that is your own team. It can be hard to overcome pride and admit that someone else has come up with a better way of doing things but if you don't bite that bullet then the business is unlikely to move on.

HERE'S AN IDEA FOR YOU...

Get your staff together and throw out a problem as a question without offering a solution. Keep quiet. If there is a free and easy discussion, good. If nobody has ideas, dares proffer them or you don't want to hear them, then you may be micromanaging and strangling your business.

11 THE DEVIL IS IN THE DETAIL

Never mind what they say – it often actually pays to sweat the small stuff because, as Franklin says, *'adviseth to circumspection and care, even in the smallest matters, because sometimes a little neglect may breed great mischief'*.

The business guru Richard Carlson was the one who advised us 'don't sweat the small stuff' but, as fine as that advice may sometimes be, it should really go straight out the window when it comes to websites, communications and all sorts of promotional material.

Back in the mid-90s the web dragged itself out of the primeval swamp of the Internet, and promptly evolved into a nerd playground complete with eye-popping games and porn. It's perhaps unsurprising, then, that the business world still retains a highly ambivalent attitude to it to this day. A great many company websites were initially knocked together by some employee's kid brother working in a back bedroom. All credit to the pioneering spirit of those armies of nascent geeks, but their legacy is that companies a) expect to pay for all sorts of webbery in pizzas and diet coke, b) impose a very different quality threshold on electronic material than they would for a printed brochure or other literature they were sending out, and c) still have terrible websites that look like they were knocked up by a sleep-deprived teenager.

Benjamin Franklin was understandably ignorant of the wonders of HTML, TCP/IP and Flash animation but he nonetheless made points that are as relevant in the digital domain as they were then. It's just that he illustrated the point with horse-shoe nails rather than pixels. *'For want of a nail the shoe was lost; for want of a shoe the horse was lost, and for want of a horse the rider was lost, being overtaken and slain by the enemy, all for want of care about a horse-shoe nail.'*

You don't have to look far online to see that the World Wide Web is liberally scattered with discarded horse-shoe nails. Senior management rarely take the time to ensure that those involved with digital media are doing their job, and it shows in such everyday nuisances as links that go nowhere and 'info@mycompany' addresses that send email enquiries straight into the inbox of, erm, nobody. Official websites for deeply respected companies sport spelling mistakes that would shame a six year old. Vague attempts at translation are so poor that they insult rather than welcome foreign visitors, probably because they're still being put together by a back-bedroom teenager who is copying the foreign language off a Wiki/Facebook/porn page in the target language.

You wouldn't print thousands of copies of a company brochure without having it carefully proofread and checked by a professional. So why broadcast to tens of thousands of visitors, potential clients and customers that you don't really care about what they think when it comes to the web?

HERE'S AN IDEA FOR YOU...

There's nothing quite as shoddy as having spelling errors in an email. Use spell checkers intelligently, and if your email programme doesn't provide a relevant one (say it's in US English and you're in the UK) then write your message in a word processor which does. Copy and paste it in.

12 KEEPING RETAIL REAL

You might think someone writing over two centuries ago wouldn't have a handle on 'retail therapy' and its problems. But Franklin did. Consider this: *'buy what thou hast no need of, and ere long thou shalt sell thy necessaries.'*

DEFINING IDEA...

Money is better than poverty, if only for financial reasons.
~ WOODY ALLEN

We have all done it. It might be the latest, shiniest i-Thingy, a company car which is this year's model or, in extreme cases, even that small but irritating rival company you've always hankered after buying out. In each case the whole purchase experience runs like a roller coaster from anticipatory nerves to orgasmic retail delight to post-retail therapy discussion. From there the excitement gradually slips away to the point where the i-Thingy sits forgotten in the back of the cupboard while you're going over the credit card bills with a growing sense of disbelief.

Retail therapy, like comfort eating and chocoholism, seems to work on a basis of binge and bust whereby once we're in the 'zone' we actually look around for more things to buy. We genuinely convince ourselves that the new sound system just isn't complete without a professional-quality mixing deck even though all we're going to use it for is listening to the Corrs while cooking. Think about how many people you know who own a top of the range shiny Scandiwegian fridge which opens to reveal a curling sandwich, a dead tomato and some curdling milk. As for buying new cars, there is no end to which we can be upsold to a better model with extras we will only ever use to demonstrate to our friends exactly how fab the vehicle is. All of which would be just fine, bog-standard human frippery if it wasn't for the annoying detail that this kind of cerebellum-numbing consumerism comes at a cost. Often it's a cost which is quietly topped up by credit card rates, which finally leads to insidious – and ultimately horrendous – debt problems.

Franklin was a great proponent of the make-do-and-mend philosophy of anti-consumerism, an attitude that has more recently come back into vogue partly as a backlash to the rampant consumerism of the 80s and 90s, and partly as a very common-sense response to the soaring levels of personal debt across most of the West. The generation which is old enough to remember rationing or double-digit interest rates almost automatically understands the make-do-and-mend approach as a way of life. The problem is that those of us who have lived through neither tend to see both credit and resources as limitless.

It matters little whether you decide to curb your consumerism on the basis of morals or budget (or budget disguised as morals), the simple truth is that a few months down the line you will almost certainly thank yourself for holding back on spending on goods that you knew, in your heart of hearts, you did not need.

HERE'S AN IDEA FOR YOU...

You want something, but you won't expire if you don't buy it. Impose a twenty-eight-day moratorium. Take out your diary, write the object and the price on today's date, and a note reminding you about it twenty-eight days later. If it still seems desirable then, perhaps it's worthwhile. You're more likely to have forgotten about it.

13 IF YOU HAVE TO SHOP, SHOP SMART

'*Who dainties love, shall beggars prove,*' said Franklin, meaning that if you pick up expensive tastes then you run the risk that they will ruin you by way of thanks.

Rampant consumerism hadn't hit home in the America of Franklin's time. He lived in an age where there wasn't much of a market for second-hand goods simply because people held on to their things until they were beyond selling or handed them down through family and friends. Then again, he didn't know the beauty of eBay, Amazon, Wiggle or comparison engines.

You may still want to buy yourself a shiny i-Thingy. Sometimes it's going to happen, but if you absolutely must have expensive tastes then at least do the smart thing and shop around before you pillage your purse.

Today, if you really, truly have to shop, you can almost always find the products cheaper direct online, or at least use a price comparison agent (such as Kelkoo) to see which retailers are currently offering the best deal. But to really get the benefit of buying online you should consider going second hand, or 'pre-owned' if you prefer the phrase.

Take a look at Amazon. I recently looked for a copy of a book that was retailing for around £16 in the shops. Sure enough, there it was on

Amazon for only about £11, a healthy reduction. But if you checked the new and used link next to the book there were good condition copies for about £6 and that kind of saving makes a difference to my weekly budget. The same approach applies to just about everything, no matter how high up the luxury scale you go. Car dealerships and classified ad newspapers might not be too happy about it, but eBay is now the biggest seller of second-hand (sorry, pre-owned) cars in the UK. Fancy a Rolex but put off by the extortionate price of this year's model? You could opt for last year's one at a hefty reduction, but something tells me that if you're into the label that much you won't be interested in last year's model. So instead try going for a classic with a little history to go with it – it's a smart and stylish alternative at a fraction of the price.

The only downside is to remember that luxury goods are plagued by the scourge of fakes. So if you're after a big-ticket item of some kind, you have to have absolute confidence in the seller. That means knowing where they are physically located and what their reputation is. Check into them and make sure they know why you are asking – a legitimate dealer will only welcome the enquiry and be happy to establish the authenticity of their goods.

HERE'S AN IDEA FOR YOU...

Some comparison engines aren't disinterested third parties, but middlemen taking commission. As such, some suppliers – the ones who only deal direct – do not deal with them. So check out www.travelsupermarket.com to find a cheap flight, but remember there might be a better offer on the site of a no-frills airline.

14 DEATH AND TAXES?

Whoever thought taxes were the only sure-fire outgoing in life clearly hadn't tried to keep a roof over their head, let alone a car on the road. Benjamin Franklin was far closer to the truth when he observed that *'gain may be temporary and uncertain, but ever while you live, expense is constant and certain'.*

Contrary to common wisdom (and to one of Franklin's other statements – check out the Defining Idea) death and taxes aren't the only sure things in life nowadays. As luck would have it, there are shedloads of expenses that are coming your way as sure as eggs is eggs.

We all know that. If we think back we all know that in any given year there will be at least one major repair or replacement bill for plumbing or something electrical or automotive, and yet every time it happens we throw up our hands in despair and wonder where on earth we're going to find the money. Chances are, it's the credit card that takes the strain and then surreptitiously siphons the money out of your life with monthly payments. Nor are businesses immune. Every business suffers 'unexpected' expenses on an annual basis with technology that needs replacing, outgoings on premises or the cost of financing fallow periods.

So how about budgeting for those entirely predictable 'unexpected' expenses?

Start off by taking an honest look over your figures for the last few years. Don't have figures? Well, there's your problem for a start. If you don't have a household budget then being surprised by entirely predictable expenses must be pretty much a way of life round your way. If we're talking about a business here, and you don't have figures, then I can only presume that you're reading this from behind bars or on a yacht in the Bahamas since the tax authorities don't look kindly on insouciance when it comes to spreadsheets.

The chances are that you can identify a pattern of expenses for which it would make sense to have a financial buffer ready. Now you'll need to find the money. So identify your annual target sum and break it down into monthly, or even weekly, contributions. Breaking saving sums into weekly contributions has two benefits: it makes them more accessible and makes you realise just how long it takes to save up enough for a 'fighting fund' for the unexpected. If you really want to balance your books, this is the time to look at your weekly outgoings and see where you could trim the expenses to create those savings. This could mean doing something as simple as cutting out a few luxuries from the weekly food basket. Think of that the next time you're staring down the business end of a chocolate doughnut. Your physical health could even benefit as well…

HERE'S AN IDEA FOR YOU…

Create a fighting fund for the expected unexpected. You can get a decent rate of interest by opening a saver account with a relatively small amount and still get instant access. Can you spare that small amount right now? If the answer is 'yes', what are you waiting for?

15 MANY A MICKLE

Franklin was no fan of finery. He believed in sticking to the basics as he made clear when observing that '*Many a one, for the sake of finery on the back, have gone with a hungry belly, and half starved their families*'.

'Many a mickle makes a muckle', as my Granny always said. There again, Gran also used to tell me that witches used empty eggshells as boats in order to sink sailors' ships, so I don't think she's going to be writing a lot of business self-help books any time soon.

The idea that little things add up is certainly not new, and Benjamin Franklin really warmed to his task when it came to warning about the accumulating costs of small expenses. 'You may think perhaps that a little tea, or a little punch now and then, diet a little more costly, clothes a little finer, and a little entertainment now and then, can be no great Matter; but remember what Poor Richard says, many a little makes a mickle, and farther, beware of little expenses; a small leak will sink a great ship.' The more I think about it the more I notice that Grandma Shipside and Benjamin share a remarkable number of common interests (let alone vocabulary).

History hasn't been kind to the frugal over the last half century or so. Those brought up in wartime or with rationing need no telling about the need for tightening belts. Those of us brought up since then have tended to rebel against the attitudes of earlier generations, swapped 'frugal' for 'penny-pinching' and enjoyed almost unfettered spending – but with that freedom has come a general loss of awareness of the cost of small things. The 'price of a pint' (of milk) test is a celebrated way of testing just how out of touch celebrities are, but you don't have to be a rock star to fail the test; most of us don't really add up what we spend on the little things in life.

There is a strong argument that it really is the small leaks that harm small businesses. That's because they have a tendency to pass unnoticed, whereas major expenses are carefully scrutinized and weighed up. When was the last time you really counted up what you spent in a week on all those little daily expenses and indulgences? Do you know exactly what your journey to work costs in petrol? I'll bet you haven't a clue. What about how much per week you spend on cappuccino, chocolate bars or sandwiches? What about those petty cash outgoings, especially the really little ones? Office coffee, tea, milk (see, told you it's not just rock stars who should take the test)? Printer toner? Copier paper? Add it all up and you'll have a muckle or two, I'll warrant. You really do need to get a grip on these things, and you need to do so now.

HERE'S AN IDEA FOR YOU...

Spend a week recording your daily spend. Break it down into transport, food, etc. Multiply upwards to see what you spend a year on each category. Add tax at the appropriate percentage, and see how much you must earn to pay for them... then look at what you could save by opting for cheaper alternatives.

16 DOWN, BUT NOT OUT

Franklin knew all about consumerism: *'when you have bought one fine thing you must buy ten more, that your appearance may be all of a piece.'* **To which his reply, or, strictly speaking, that of his character Poor Dick, is to observe that** *'… 'tis easier to suppress the first desire than to satisfy all that follow it'.*

This is actually the seed from which the whole downshifting ethos springs. Have you considered that real wealth may come by rejecting the pursuit of money altogether, or at least toning down its role in your life? While Franklin didn't specifically discuss downsizing, he certainly touched on the idea at its core.

All too often consumerism becomes a form of financial arms race with your peers. Let's face it, did you really aspire to this year's model of car back when none of your friends had a car at all? Keeping up with the Joneses is seen as a joke, a quintessentially suburban pastime. The sad truth, however, is that while we don't think we indulge, we are all keeping up with the Joneses to some degree. Whether it's to gain social acceptance ('all the other kids have a pony'), to reassure ourselves of success ('Dad never drove a Jag') or the more obvious forms of rivalry, we are constantly buying more and more things in an endless escalation.

If you can deconstruct the arms race bit by bit, stripping away the need for the new car or the cruise to Aruba, you eventually get to the point where you realise you don't need that job at all and could very easily double your leisure time, spend more of it with the kids and breathe fresh air somewhere far away from your curtain-twitching neighbours.

The trick is to be aware that there is a major difference between running towards and running away. If your only real driving motive is fleeing your current life then you're not even close to being able to realise your dream. You have to carefully consider how you're going to support yourself (and your family), and how that matches your actual needs.

What's often forgotten is the fact that your new life must now give you enough personal satisfaction to replace the ego-boosts and backslapping that salary, perks and shiny things provided in your old life. Be realistic about what it is you're going to do. If your downshifting dreams dwell almost entirely on a pastoral idyll that you've never actually experienced then you're likely to run into some hard facts about your new life and its budget. Moving into an area you don't really know will also bring risks of resistance from locals who won't appreciate being appropriated as a backdrop for your fantasies; you'll need to become part of rural life.

HERE'S AN IDEA FOR YOU...

Instead of running off to become a chicken farmer, why not try to outsource yourself and work part time or freelance? Keeping a foot in the door of your old job while taking a step back is a stretch, but it's a way of seeing if the new balance suits you.

17 WORLD WIDE TIMEWASTER

'But dost thou love life, then do not squander time, for that's the stuff life is made of.' So goes one of the many exhortations to time saving that pepper _The Way to Wealth_.

Humankind has come up with all sorts of ways of wasting time. Bureaucracy, test cricket, bubblewrap – but nothing, nothing, comes close to the web when it comes to lost hours.

One suspects that if Franklin had been forced to face Outlook, Facebook and Stick Man Cricket (you haven't tried it?) he would have thrown up his hands in horror. Hours and hours of our precious lives seem to disappear in front of screens and keyboards, and often with precious little to show for it.

Some companies have fought back, of course, and Carphone Warehouse even experimented with banning email altogether. Many companies with the technical know-how to implement it have introduced proxy servers delivering a choice selection of Internet Lite rather than give their staff direct access to the distractions of the real deal. Neither of these solutions, however, tends to suit the self-employed person or small-business owner.

Well, there is always self-discipline; impose a single half-hour slot to deal with email at the beginning and end of the working day, and only allow yourself a general surfing break at lunchtime. The problem is that self-discipline tends to be up there with common sense as one of those things that it's much easier to preach about than to put into practice. Or you could always ignore the problem and go quietly into denial as your life slips gently down the digital drain, sucked away by hours of sifting emails, replying to social networking queries and playing pointless online games (did I mention Stick Man Cricket?).

If self-discipline just isn't working for you, then you could come clean, admit you have the work ethic of a child and treat yourself accordingly. There are a number of software packages that allow parents to set up profiles for their kids which limit their Internet access to a certain number of websites and block surfing to unspecified ones. Install one of these and use it to create different log-on profiles with different privileges. One should be your 'parent' mode in which you can waste your time on whatever takes your fancy, and one should be your 'work' profile which blocks access to anything other than the site(s) you need to access for work. That way, when you sign on for work you can't be sidetracked into following that hilarious link your friend sent you – or at least not unless you decide to sign out of your work mode, sign back in as yourself and then go and check it out. Because doing all this means actively switching out of work mode to waste time, it should help reinforce the fact that you are now squandering your time (and thus, ultimately, your life).

HERE'S AN IDEA FOR YOU...

Go to www.download.com and type in 'parental control'. You'll find a hoard of free or free-to-try filters. What you're looking for is not so much one that handles black (banned) lists but one that handles white lists – approved sites. With an administrator setting and parental controls you can rein in your inner child.

18 INVEST IN YOUR NUMBER ONE ASSET: YOU

A Renaissance man of the first order, Franklin believed you worked you way to wealth by means of your own skill and nothing else – or as he put it *'then help hands, for I have no lands, or if I have, they are smartly taxed'*.

Some of us hated school and spent most of our college years drinking and chasing the opposite sex (you too, huh?). Only accountants continue to take exams after that, right? Day courses are for ladies who lunch; evening courses for people who never learnt to read or write. Wrong, wrong, wrong.

DEFINING IDEA...

Don't waste time learning the 'tricks of the trade'. Instead, learn the trade.

~ TRADITIONAL SAYING

Education doesn't stop because you got a degree. Or because you didn't. We're all learning as we go, and anyone who wants to make themselves marketable and successful will look for ways of consolidating that learning into skills or qualifications that are recognisable and understandable to others. As Franklin puts it *'he that hath a trade hath an estate'*, meaning that if you have a skill that others want then you have a solid foundation of your own on which to build. Which is fine if you're a plumber or a piano tuner, but a tad more tricky if you're a consultant or work in communications.

Trades just aren't as clear-cut as they used to be for a number of reasons. One is that Western societies have moved away from pushing products and are instead increasingly focused on providing services. Services tend to be a bit more nebulous and so are the job titles and roles that go with them. Another is that jobs exist that have simply never existed before. I used to think I knew what an evangelist was but I had to re-think after meeting a growing number of Technology Evangelists and even Games Evangelists. For a while I myself gloried in the job title of The Naked Guy (not half as much fun as it sounds) and was in charge of podcasting, blogs and Wikis.

This fast-changing workscape, however, only serves to underline the importance of one of the staples of having a trade, which is having demonstrable skills. If the fruit of your labours is a product you always have the luxury of simply pointing at it and saying 'I do that, me'. If, as is increasingly the case, the fruit of your labours is far harder to pin down then you might want to think about qualifications or vocational training which can add weight to your claim that you know what you're doing.

Further education doesn't have to be something that takes place in a classroom, either. Remote learning has boomed with the advent of the web and even old favourites like the UK's Open University have taken to such modern joys as digital seminars over the Net. Which makes it harder than ever to say you don't have the time or the opportunity to add to your qualifications.

HERE'S AN IDEA FOR YOU...

No accreditation for your trade or industry? Create one. Bespoke accreditation schemes from bodies such as the British Accreditation Bureau can be drawn up to establish credible standards for any industry or area of business. Creating a standard and complying with it is a great way of raising yourself above the competition.

19 EATING THE ELEPHANT

Don't be daunted by big tasks – instead break them down to a manageable size. As the man said, *''Tis true there is much to be done, and perhaps you are weak handed, but stick to it steadily, and you will see great effects…'*

In South Africa there's a saying which goes 'How do you eat an elephant?' to which the answer is 'One spoonful at a time.' This simply means that any apparently daunting task can be dealt with effectively by breaking it down into much smaller components and tackling those one at a time.

Franklin, as far as I am aware, didn't go in for elephant analogies. However, he did drum home the elephant/spoon issue not once but repeatedly and chose a number of other analogies to make his point: '…for constant dripping wears away stones, and by diligence and patience the mouse ate in two the cable; and little strokes fell great oaks.'

Of course, in day-to-day life you may not choose to see yourself as a cable-chewing rodent, let alone a drip, but the essential idea is this: don't be daunted by the size of a task. Instead break it down, identify what you can do, what you can't do, what help you need and where your own personal efforts will have the most effect in getting the job done.

A friend of mine works as a trouble-shooting consultant for global media projects that are starting to look as though they are going decidedly fruit-shaped. Time and time again, she tells me, the real cause of the problem is not individual incompetence but rather a form of group hysteria. The sheer vastness of the job at hand leaves the people involved feeling impotent and squandering precious time as the inevitable deadline approaches.

Her first step is to call everyone to heel and break the job down into:
- Objectives;
- Deadline;
- Target audience;
- Our stakeholders (and their needs/goals);
- Their stakeholders (ditto).

Having laid out all these key areas, the next step is to drill down into each one in turn, examining it in a lot more detail. Now the team can focus on the effect that the category 'objectives', for example, has on something like the content, design and function of websites. That, in turn, leads neatly on to a discussion of the disciplines needed (which could be technical, creative, strategy, planning and media in this example) in order to get the whole project off the ground. As often as not, it is at this point that it becomes clear exactly what outside help is needed and precisely which roles should fall to which people or teams. With everyone much more assured of what their individual responsibility is, the whole job starts to slowly rumble forwards – and people stop running around in circles like clockwork mice and get on with chewing that cable.

HERE'S AN IDEA FOR YOU...

If you're given an elephant to eat it's often because someone higher up has looked at it and decided they're not hungry. Don't procrastinate; break the job down. If you can come up with a reason why at least part of it is really the responsibility of those further up you can delegate upwards.

20 DO BE DO BE DO...

Franklin is no friend of procrastinators. One of the recurrent themes of *The Way to Wealth* is the need to get on the case right now and not put things off. *'Work while it is called today, for you know not how much you may be hindered tomorrow,'* he intones.

This is all very well in an ideal world. Sometimes, however, you have no choice but to leave some items of work until tomorrow, perhaps because those kids aren't going to pick themselves up from school, or perhaps because the alternative is to run screaming from the building and security have already warned you about doing that. In these circumstances – and in many others – the simple to-do list can become your friend.

Now, some people see to-do lists as just a means of putting things off. After all, it's a lot easier to write down items on a to-do list than it is to actually do the things you have written on it. Others baulk at to-do lists simply because once you start detailing everything you're supposed to be working on, there is a strong impulse to fake your own death or run away to sea, or both. However, for the true to-do blackbelts there is a mastery and mythology about the to-do list that repays the effort of learning.

Typically people compile their to-do lists in the morning, often as a way of putting off actually starting work. If it helps you to organise your day then that's not in itself a bad thing, but it is often far more productive to write your list at the end of the day when the pressing tasks and problems are far more fresh in your mind. On top of that, you'll be more relaxed about the tasks that you have already committed to your to-do list, as the act of organising your thoughts and writing your list calms you down. It helps you to focus on the next day, while also helping to ensure the good night's sleep you will need to deal with that day to come. So finish your day with a today/tomorrow to-do list.

Don't just jumble everything up in the list like a shopping list; prioritise the order of tasks by grading them depending on exactly how critical it is that they be done on that particular day. You can use an A, B, C or a traffic-light colour-coding system, as you wish, but make sure that the end result is visually clear – those truly important items should leap right off the list at you when you scan it, even in passing. Finally, be careful about that grading when carrying items over to the next to-do list. Don't just copy it without thinking, as items which were unimportant on one day may well end up being time critical in another day or so.

HERE'S AN IDEA FOR YOU...

Your to-do list can shield you from those delegating task dumpers. Any delegated task must find not only a slot in your to-do list but a grading. If its grading doesn't put it at the top of the list, point that out to the would-be task dumper and refuse.

21 BE PHYSICALLY FIT ENOUGH TO EARN A FORTUNE

When Franklin tells us that *'sloth, by bringing on diseases, absolutely shortens life'* he's not referring to upside-down South American mammals – he means that couch potatoes will vacate their seats on the board earlier than their more active colleagues.

DEFINING IDEA...

A country can truly call itself sporting when the majority of its people feel a personal need for sport.

~ PIERRE DE COUBERTIN, FATHER OF THE MODERN OLYMPIC GAMES

If physical fitness was the key to wealth then Bill Gates would be taking investment advice from Chuck Norris and FTSE 100 boardrooms would be filled with ripped, lean torsos and buttocks of steel. If you snorted milk out of your nose on reading that then you've seen the kind of people who sit in FTSE 100 boardrooms. Clearly physical fitness isn't a necessity for earning a fortune, and the truly wealthy are more likely to look like The Simpsons' Montgomery Burns than David Beckham, but that doesn't mean that fitness is unimportant to success.

Unless you've been living under a rock for the last decade you already know that you should be exercising for half an hour or more at least three times a week. What you might have missed was that this does more than trim your waistline and give grown men an excuse to wear tights in public. In addition to improving lung and heart capacity which, in themselves, may add years to your life and improve your daily lot, exercise has a number of benefits that affect wealth as well as health.

Physical fitness is proven to help cope with stress. Left untreated, extreme stress can bring on anxiety, tense muscles, high blood pressure and low resistance to illness. Non-competitive sports help counter all of the above as well as boosting your immune system to make you more resilient to illness. By releasing endorphins in the body, exercise also makes you feel good; it's been shown to help with anxiety and depression. A sensible fitness regime also helps you sleep better, which in turn has a beneficial effect on both productivity and stress levels. Plus there is the psychological effect that because fitness and activity increase self-esteem, they can also build self-confidence.

Put together, all that means that someone who exercises sensibly on a regular basis is likely to be sharper, better rested, more able to deal with stress, less likely to fall ill and more productive than someone whose idea of exercise is changing the channel using the remote. But before you bellow at your workforce to drop and give you twenty, just remember that this applies every bit as much to you.

By far the best exercise is that which you incorporate into your life, rather than which you take time out of life to do. If you want to get wealthy, and better yet stick around long enough to enjoy that wealth, then you'd better stop making snide remarks about the sweaties in sports clothes and instead get out and join them.

HERE'S AN IDEA FOR YOU...

Look for ways to bring sport into your life. That could mean transport — switch to walking or cycling instead of driving — or trying something social like five-a-side footie or tennis. You're more likely to keep it up if you do it with others. Check out the options and move that body.

22 QUALITY TIME

'Leisure is time for doing something useful; this leisure the diligent man will obtain, but the lazy man never,' said Franklin, taking leisure seriously.

We associate the idea of quality time with the time-starved, work-obsessed West Coast Americans trying desperately to tend to their neglected relationships, families and personal lives. Back in the 1750s Franklin was already on the case.

Although much is made of Franklin's repeated calls to industry and frugality, it's often overlooked that he also rated leisure seriously enough to distinguish between quality leisure time and wasted time. He was an advocate of taking your leisure seriously and using it for something more constructive than vegging out in front of reality TV while tucking into tortilla chips. Not that he personally suffered from the twin plagues of Big Brother and barbecue sauce-flavoured chips, but from the general tone of *The Way to Wealth* it's a fair inference that he wouldn't have approved of either.

If you're flat out at work the idea that you need to do more with your leisure time might sound like madness but in fact it makes perfect sense. Doing nothing sounds like bliss when you're busy and stressed, but in fact doing nothing is not the antidote to stress – far from it. If you can't clear your mind of work then your downtime is likely to become an extension of your working worries, and a festering, stagnating extension of them at that.

Speaking personally, I know that as someone who works from home I have to make a special effort to get away from my work, so I really do try to get out more. That doesn't mean pubbing and clubbing all the time (not quite, anyway), it means outdoor sports, meeting up with friends to try new hobbies, lots of short breaks away from home and plenty of travel. That doesn't mean I can't relax at home; far from it. I have sacred relaxation rituals ('hammock time') but these are special moments set aside. What I try not to do is lose time to the TV or the sofa. That doesn't mean I don't watch TV or slouch happily with a book; it's just that I try to choose what to watch or when to chill. I almost never switch off at the end of the night with the vaguely unsettling feeling that I've just been suckered into watching three hours of junk the way you might walk away from an all-you-can-eat buffet wondering why you did it. However, I'll admit that I only got to this stage after years of losing my life to wasted moments.

Benjamin F. spotted a long way back that the only real way to relax from work is not to do nothing, but to go out and do something completely different. Dynamic downtime is more satisfying, refreshing, rich and, above all, easier to share.

HERE'S AN IDEA FOR YOU...

Take the plunge. Grab a listings magazine, check online – however you find it, pick something you've never done before and do it this weekend. It doesn't have to be hang-gliding; how about a foreign language class or a guerrilla-gardening outing? See how refreshing it can be to do something fresh.

23 TACKLE THOSE TIME THIEVES

Where lots of other writers dwell dreamily on the possibilities of 'Tomorrow', our Benjamin was a resolute 'Today' man: *'One today is worth two tomorrows.'* Make the most of your today.

Welcome to today. It might be raining, you might have a tough one ahead, but whatever the case this is the only time you're going to see this day. You'll never get it back. So why let someone steal it from you?

DEFINING IDEA...

You cannot step twice into the same river.
~ HERACLITUS OF EPHESUS

There are lots of time thieves out there: institutional thieves that make you wait or jump through hoops, corporate thieves that treat you as one of millions and rank your time accordingly, and individual thieves who either steal your time to add to theirs or else purloin and waste it because they don't know any better. Learn to spot them and snatch a bit of your time back for yourself.

Institutions, be they public or corporate, are the hardest to battle. Statisticians tell us that we spend around forty-five minutes of every day waiting for something. PDAs, mobile phones and the dreaded BlackBerry maybe known as digital leashes for their role in tying people to their jobs, but there's no question that they come into their own when it comes to reclaiming dead time. The exec calmly ordering emails while waiting in line would be an enviable sight if it wasn't for the fact that you know they'll still be doing emails late at night. You don't need technology to thwart time thieves, though. Just be prepared. Read those briefing notes, take notes of your own, just make sure you're never ever sitting/standing there with nothing to do but wait.

Individual time thieves are both more insidious and easier to deal with. Insidious, because you may not even notice that they're stealing your life, but easier to deal with because (unlike institutions) you have the power to shape their behaviour. Some thieves are deliberate – they're trying to hijack your time so they have less to do themselves. More often, though, thieves don't even realise they're doing it – like the insecure colleague who insists on talking through all their dilemmas in the hope that you'll make up their mind for them, or the person who wants to talk about some meeting you're only peripherally involved in but which is very important to them.

In which case don't just nod and watch your own time slip away – explain in a friendly but firm way that you have a rush job right now but what they're saying sounds very important, so they should jot down the key points in an email/memo for you and you'll look at it. This does two things. The first is that true time thieves will never actually write down their musings because it seems like work, and the second is that deliberators will often come to their own conclusions when they set their thoughts down on paper (or screen).

HERE'S AN IDEA FOR YOU...

If someone wants to talk about a document, development or agenda insist they send it to you first. If you allow them to discuss it before you see it, they'll try to paint the whole thing in their own words (needlessly, since it already exists) or colour it with their agenda.

24 MAKING THE MOST OF YOUR WORKING WEEK

'Employ thy time well if thou meanest to gain leisure,' said Benjamin and I, for one, take that to mean don't spend days of your life sitting in rock-solid traffic.

Let's presume for a moment that your work is rewarding, challenging and deeply pleasurable with nary a wasted moment. It's a stretch I know, but work with me. Even if all the above is true then it's pretty much a certainty that there's one major part of your working day that is, at best, dead time… the commute.

Naturally there will be somebody out there who is carried to work in a sedan chair borne aloft by a bevy of attractive members of the opposite sex. That person is disagreeing with this right now. For the rest of us, crammed into late trains or sitting in traffic, the commute is one of the worst parts of the day. It doesn't take long to do the maths. If you spend about a hour each way getting to work then you're losing the equivalent of a working day a week sitting, stressing, swearing – and, what's even worse, paying for the privilege. So how about working from home instead?

Strictly speaking, I'd advise you to avoid the phrase 'working from home' because to management ears that sounds indistinguishable from the 'food poisoning' so often suffered on Monday mornings. Indeed the biggest single problem of anyone who wants to stop wasting their time on transport is that they are immediately seen as a time waster. It's as if you have to pay your dues with hours of cramped travel in order to be seen to really want your job.

That doesn't have to be the case, however. The advent of email, broadband-equipped home computers and such technological marvels as Virtual Private Networks means that to a corporate network you are as present (absent?) at home as you are in the office – as long as you are logged on and working. Furthermore, many governments are now formally encouraging people to try flexible working, partly in response to the fact that long hours and both parents slogging away in offices aren't seen to be in line with those family values so dear to politicians.

Few companies have a culture flexible enough to suddenly swallow full-scale flexible working, so don't try and force it down your particular company's throat. Try instead to secure yourself just one or two days a week, and make it clear that this means being online and on duty for the whole day or you'll be perceived as a part timer. If you're going to argue for a day of home working, then make sure you have agreed goals for that day's work with your boss. These should be crystal clear and deliverable, rather than vague generalisations about being contactable.

HERE'S AN IDEA FOR YOU...

Take the initiative with your boss and note down the normal workload you achieve in the office and agree to deliver it from home. But be careful: if you're not that productive normally, you'll be bringing this to your boss' attention. Not a good idea, so prepare the ground first.

25 IT'S NOT A GOOD TIME

Franklin actually wants us to reverse the rot and do tomorrow's work today. At least that's what he says: *'Have you somewhat to do tomorrow, do it today'…*

That sounds a bit ambitious – until you consider that really it's a sneaky way of Franklin making his point about procrastination again in a slightly different way. By exhorting us to take on tomorrow's work today he's really just trying to strike back at the way work tends to get mugged by that mañana spirit.

DEFINING IDEA…

Procrastination is opportunity's assassin.
~ VICTOR KIAM, THE MAN WHO LIKED THE RAZOR SO MUCH HE BOUGHT THE COMPANY

It's particularly unfair that we opt for a Spanish word to portray procrastination since it's pretty much a way of life for most of us. In fact in our household I don't think I would ever get round to doing the washing up if it wasn't for the occasional writing deadline. Let's say the washing up is all done, however; you've polished the windows, done the ironing and cleaned the mouthpiece of the phone handset. You're running out of things to do and there is that sneaking suspicion that you might be putting something off. Now is time to try to figure out why.

The most likely reason is that the job in question is one you don't want to do. It might be hard, it might be scary, but whatever it is you'd rather see if somebody else could make the bad thing go away. That's natural enough, but instead of waiting and hoping you have to either decide if you're just being work-shy or whether the putting off is down to a fear that the task is too big to handle. In which case, don't wait for someone to make it go away; either hire someone to do the job or delegate it to someone else.

First, be honest with yourself about the difference between a genuine decision to delay doing something (because conditions will be more appropriate at a later date) and an irrational postponement.

Then think about these points:

- Consider if you can break the job down into bite-sized morsels and tackle those one at a time.

- Is indecision plaguing you? If so, lay out the criteria as you see them and set a deadline for the decision.

- Afraid of failing? Afraid of success? Try not to focus on the task or your fear but instead on visualising the finished task and the rewards this will bring either in itself, in time freed for other things or in relief that it's all over.

- Can you really not be bothered? If you don't care about it then ask yourself why this task has fallen to you. It could be that you do care, really, but have lost sight of the goal (personal, financial, etc.). Or it could be that you have nothing invested in this job and perhaps somebody else would be better suited to take it on. You know it can't be right to hog something you don't want to do.

HERE'S AN IDEA FOR YOU...

If you realise that it's just a question of rolling up your sleeves and getting on with it, then pick a time for the job right now. Make sure you're not going to be distracted — because you know you'll be more than happy to abandon something you've put off this long.

26 YOU SNOOZE... YOU WIN!

'Plenty of time to sleep when you're dead', say clubbers, rad dudes and candle-burners generally, but few of them realise that Benjamin Franklin beat them to it by more than a couple of centuries when he said *'there will be sleeping enough in the grave'.*

However, Franklin probably didn't mean that it was cool to fuel your all-nighters with Red Bull and vodka – but he did have a horror of wasted time and argued strongly that *'how much more than is necessary do we spend in sleep! Forgetting that the sleeping fox catches no poultry'.*

Modern foxes may be interested to know that research suggests that while the brain definitely needs some occasional down time, it almost certainly doesn't require ten hours of one-to-one with the duvet. In actual fact short 'power naps' of twenty or thirty minutes are probably all you need to refresh the grey matter and power up your productivity accordingly. NASA researchers have found that a thirty-minute power nap resulted in better scores from volunteers taking IQ tests as a gauge of mental agility. The results were quite marked – their scores were up to 40% better, in fact.

Power-napping proponents also point to lower stress rates and incidence of heart disease amongst those who regularly practise the art. None of this will surprise people who come from Latin cultures, for whom the siesta has long been seen as an essential part of the daily routine. The benefits of a siesta will also be immediately apparent to anyone who has had to present something important – or indeed, anything – to that first meeting after lunch.

All of this should not be seen as an excuse for the chronically lazy among us, however, as most research suggests that there is an upper limit to the length of a nap for optimum effectiveness. After about forty-five minutes you might well still be snugly asleep but you're not doing any more to boost your brain.

There is one major downside to the power nap, however, which is persuading your colleagues that you are in fact upping your productivity rather than slacking off like Homer Simpson. Whilst there are one or two work environments that have accepted the power nap, you may find that your particular boss takes a dim view of it. If you're lucky enough to have a boss who sports a droopy moustache, an oversized sombrero and a poncho then try suggesting a snooze lounge for tag-team napping.

And if you have no success, and you don't have a dedicated snooze room, there's even a thing called an Executive Hammock which is a tiny nylon fold-away hammock intended for use in the office, maybe strung up between the filing cabinets. Or if you can't find a suitable fixing point then you could simply have two flunkies hold up the ends while you refresh yourself…

HERE'S AN IDEA FOR YOU…

There are phone/iPod-friendly mp3 files specifically for snoozing along to. These consist of twenty or thirty minutes of white noise (intended to help drown out external sound) followed by a series of gentle waking noises to bring you back from the land of nod. Search online for free samples; try www.placebo.serv.co.za/?page_id=7.

27 THE ART OF THE TART; RATE TART QUICK START

'The borrower is a slave to the lender', as Franklin put it and as the credit crunch starts to kick in, a great many of us are just learning the real truth of that.

DEFINING IDEA...

Money is just the poor man's credit card.
~ MARSHALL MCLUHAN

It's not just that money has been cheap to come by, but it has also been relatively easy. Cheap, meaning interest rates have been low – not many of us can remember double-figure interest rates, for example. Easy, in that credit companies have been all but battering down our doors in the rush to lend us money whether we need it or not.

Those rates are going up, though. I'm willing to bet you don't know the exact rate your lender is charging on your credit card so go and find out – banks tend to bury the bad news a little, but somewhere on that corporate website it will say what the current rate is. Found it? More than it used to be or than you thought it was? Thought so, which means that if you're not a rate tart yet then it's time to pucker up.

'Rate tart' is the term for somebody who keeps their borrowing cheap by constantly moving their credit card balance around to take advantage of 0% interest deals from new cards. A few years ago this was relatively easy, as just about every bank was offering 0% for nine months or so, but a couple of details have now come in to blot that picture.

The first is the story that constantly applying for new cards spoils your credit rating and makes it harder to get a loan. That appears to be untrue. While credit ratings do take account of the number of times you apply for credit, they also treat balance transfers as paying off the old debt. So as long as you don't do it too often (more than once or twice a year, for example) and as long as you're successful in each application, then you should be fine.

The second point is that the truly great offers of extended and catch-free 0% deals have melted away a bit as the banks have tended to pull their horns in and look for liquidity. They're still out there, however, so this just means looking around a bit more to find the right one.

The third development is that more and more transfers are subject to a fee, either as a fixed cost or as a percentage of the balance being transferred. This isn't a disaster as long as you bear it in mind and do the maths.

The art of the rate tart is not dead, but it is getting harder – which means you have to shop around more carefully with calculator in hand. Above all, remember that banks make their money when the free period ends and the punitive rates start – so red-pencil that diary date and either have the debt paid or moved before D-day.

HERE'S AN IDEA FOR YOU...

Good research is the secret to the art of the rate tart. If you want a short cut to the current deals worth moving your balance for, then have a look at the credit card section of comparison websites like www.moneysupermarket.com. Hit the search engines and find one that is relevant to you.

28 D-DAY

Once upon a time you probably thought the worst date you could forget was your anniversary. That would have been before you missed that repayment date. As Franklin said: *'creditors are a superstitious sect, great observers of set days and times.'* It pays to stay on the right side of those superstitions.

Forget your anniversary and you're in for an orgy of flouncing, slammed doors, industrial-strength sulking and whiny tears. That's presuming your partner is a man. You think that's bad? Try forgetting a bank payment.

DEFINING IDEA...

If you make a couple of late payments on a new card with an introductory rate, …your annual percentage rate could jump as much as fifteen percentage points.

~ KEN MCELDOWNEY, CONSUMER EXPERT

You may have read that the charges imposed for late payments in the UK have been lowered to a flat fee of £12 by the Office of Fair Trading after a nationwide campaign against unfair and potentially illegal fees being charged by lenders. Excellent news.

You might even be tempted to think that the new £12 is so reasonable that it's almost worth it to run a little late when things get tight come repayment time. Think again.

Every late payment will be noted on your credit record and will be seen as an indication that you are struggling with your existing level of debt.

That will mean a reassessment of your creditworthiness, so it can also affect your APR and monthly minimum repayment sums. You almost certainly didn't read all the small print when signing up for that shiny new card or balance transfer but most likely the agreement you signed included the right of the lender to assess and adjust both interest rates and monthly minimums as you go, depending on your financial behaviour.

On the same basis a card issuer may decide to reduce your current credit limit on the grounds that it is already beyond you. In extreme cases they could recall the debt altogether – and you simply can't afford to pay off that debt in one go. (If you can, then what are you doing making those late payments?)

That then has the knock-on effect that your chances of future borrowing will be reduced. Which could really hurt when you try to get a mortgage (or a remortgage if things are getting really tough). This, of course, means that your 'cheap' fee could be one of the most expensive financial choices you ever opt for.

So don't miss your payments, wherever you are, and don't try to bury your head in the sand. If you realise that the money just won't be there to pay that direct debit then get in touch with your lenders immediately. If you are seen to be acting responsibly there should be no problem working out a new schedule of repayments, and possibly a repayment 'holiday' during which you take a break from those regular payments until your financial situation improves.

HERE'S AN IDEA FOR YOU...

Go a step further than direct debits to sort out your regular outgoings. Open an instant-access savings account with the amount needed to cover one month's repayments. That's both your buffer and your alarm. The month you transfer the buffer to pay them is the signal to talk to your lender.

29 KNOW THE SCORE

'Creditors have better memories than debtors,' observed Franklin. These days it's not so much about memory per se as records. Your personal tally takes the form of your credit rating.

Fortunately it's no longer so hard to get a peek at your credit rating.

Credit reports are financial records kept by the credit reference agencies (like Experian, Equifax and Callcredit) to help lenders decide whether you're a good risk or not. This is done with your consent (it's in the small print when you apply) and the information is available for you to check at any time. The report is personal – it doesn't include details of your wayward brother unless a formal financial link has been made and, despite what we all once believed, there is no blacklist. In fact, credit reference agencies don't give you a credit score at all.

That's done by individual lenders who assign their own points system to the information on the record and tot up the total to achieve a 'pass' mark on which they base their decision. Different lenders have different points systems, so one might decide to give you credit and another could refuse you – though both use the same information. You might also be offered credit at a different rate to your mate who applied for exactly the same thing. A look at your credit report should help demystify the dark workings of the lenders.

Nor is a 'no' the end of the story. You can ask a lender about the way they tot up a credit score and if you are refused they should tell you why. These days the scoring is very likely to be done by a computer, in which case you can ask the lender to take another look at your application using a manual system. Be prepared to supply further information to support your claim.

You can also take some simple steps to improving your own record. Credit reference agencies have the right to charge a fee for revealing your details but Experian UK and Ireland is currently offering a free sample service online so you can check your reference information through their website (www.experian.co.uk). Take a look at it and see what might be the problem. Remember that while creditors do indeed have better memories than debtors, they don't remember for ever and some negative points are automatically removed after a period of time. Similarly, each time you ask for credit a record is made but that only stays on your file for two years with Equifax and Callcredit and only one year with Experian. You may also up your score simply by getting a bit older, so patience can pay.

HERE'S AN IDEA FOR YOU…

Different countries, different rules. In the UK you can improve your score just by joining the electoral register, so do it. In the US you can balance your cards to bring down the average limit – four credit cards at 25% of their limit gives a better score than three nearly paid off and one out of control.

30 SAVING THE DAY

For all that Franklin talked about working hard he was explicit about the fact that hard work alone does not necessarily mean wealth. *'A man may, if he knows not how to save as he gets, keep his nose all his life to the grindstone, and die not worth a groat at last.'*

Learn to save your groats, and buy your nose a break from that grindstone.

DEFINING IDEA...

Blessed are the young, for they shall inherit the national debt.

~ HERBERT HOOVER, ON WHY YOU NEED TO PROTECT YOUR EARNINGS FROM TAX

Savings often seem like a luxury that you simply can't afford. It's hard enough to find the money to get by, let alone the money to put by. But that's a false economy because your regular outgoings are only part of the story and sooner or later you're going to be on the receiving end of a far larger demand. Savings are also a way of taking a firm grip on outgoings and showing them who's boss. Holidays, for example, often swallow all your available cash (but hey, you deserve it, right?) and stop you making any further savings, but if you take it just a bit easy this year you could put the money saved aside for next year's holiday. That way you have a year to profit from the rising interest rates and add that extra sum to your holiday spend – and tax free if you're smart about it.

Don't underestimate the importance of ensuring savings are tax free, either. If you're in the UK and paying tax at the higher (40%) rate then £9,000 will earn £495 in interest over a year at a rate of 5.5%. The same sum in a savings account paying the same rate would only earn £297 after tax. The easiest way of (legally) dodging the tax is to use ISAs (Individual Savings Accounts) which allow a limited sum to be stashed away every year without incurring tax and without it even being declared on tax returns. Do be careful if you intend to use that cash in the next year or so, however. The ISAs offered by major UK banks are sometimes postal accounts which means that while you could theoretically take out money whenever you need it, you won't get your hands on it half as fast as you would with an online ISA.

Now, if you used to be confused about all that mini/maxi ISA stuff then you'll be glad to know that ISAs have been simplified so that from now on (the 2008/9 tax year) the annual maximum you can put into an ISA rises from £3,000 to £3,600. You can also hold shares under an equity ISA to bring your total tax-free ISA value up to £7,200 a year. You don't pay tax on the dividend payments if the shares are held in an ISA and again you don't have to bother with all that fiddly declaration stuff on your tax return.

HERE'S AN IDEA FOR YOU...

In the UK, different banks offer better ISA deals but they traditionally haven't allowed transfers. Close an old ISA to remove the cash and it loses ISA status so you're locked in. This may be changing – check out Icesave, an Icelandic provider which is shaking up the market by targeting transfers from high street banks.

31 NOT SAVING BUT DROWNING

'If you would be wealthy think of saving as well as of getting,' says Franklin. While he clearly advocates saving he adds a subtle point that modern savers would be wise to heed: *'the Indies have not made Spain rich, because her outgoes are greater than her incomes.'*

DEFINING IDEA...

People working in the private sector should try to save money. There remains the possibility that it may someday be valuable again.

~ NORMAN R. AUGUSTINE, US AEROSPACE BOSS AND AUTHOR OF AUGUSTINE'S LAWS

Outgoings exceeding incomings is an obvious recipe for financial disaster, but often we simply don't see that this is what's happening to us because we are blinded by names. It's only human, after all, to think that any money put into a savings account counts as savings. That's often not the case, however, since many of us have money in savings accounts that we virtuously refuse to raid while still running up credit card debts that are being charged at up to five times the APR of our savings. In that case a savings account is nothing of the kind – it's really a losings account.

Clearly, then, the first step towards saving is to pay off any debts that aren't being lent at a true 0% interest rate. That's a hard bullet to bite because it means that your savings disappear instantly into the pit of your outgoings, but without overcoming that psychological hurdle you'll never claw your way back into real profit.

The next step is to take a long hard look at your savings account and what it really offers. There are two main ways in which savings end up as outgoings and they can both be avoided. The first is tax. If your money isn't protected by some kind of tax-free umbrella then any interest it earns will count as taxable income.

If you still think a savings account is the way to go, or if you have already reached your tax-free limit for a given year, then make sure that it is at the highest rate possible to minimise the thieving of the second great savings stealer – inflation. Remember that when hunting for great rates, the worst place to look is almost certainly your own bank. Banks tend to reward loyal customers by doing the dirty on them when they're not looking. They rarely offer the best deals because they don't have to – they have a semi-captive audience of existing customers who use them for savings accounts and other financial products because that seems easiest.

Don't let inertia steal your precious savings; shop around and be prepared to be adventurous because the best offers are usually from places you haven't heard of. For example, in the UK at the time of writing the best deal is a savings account from Kaupthing Edge. Who?! Precisely. Unless you're a fan of Icelandic finance, Kaupthing Edge has probably passed you by. It's signed up to the UK Banking Code, though, so if it disappeared tomorrow up to £35,000 of your savings would be safe.

HERE'S AN IDEA FOR YOU...

The best deal available at any one time varies from month to month so be prepared to move your money at any time to make the most of it (introductory offers often end after a fixed period). To save surfing all the bank websites, use comparison agents.

32 DON'T GET BOGGED DOWN IN THE BAD TIMES

Everyone knows the saying 'fail to plan and you are planning to fail' but when times get tough it can be easy to forget to plan for better periods to come. Or, as Franklin put it, *'remember Job suffered, and was afterwards prosperous'.*

You don't actually have to endure a plague of boils to feel like the blues have got you and there's no way out. The realisation that you're in debt, that it's rising and you have no visible way of paying it off will usually do the trick. The good news is that there is always help on hand and there are ways out. The bad news is that some short-term solutions can actually turn out to be long-term nightmares that will seriously damage your future success. In particular, beware of Individual Voluntary Arrangements (IVAs) if you're in the UK.

You've probably seen adverts for IVAs on the TV. They tend heavily towards imagery of those drowning in debt or being locked in until miraculously they are freed of all their constraints and their debts just go away. In reality an IVA is a formal agreement between debtors and creditors where debts are frozen. Instead the debtor pays off a fixed sum every month for a fixed period (often five years). If the debtor honours that commitment, the rest of the debt is written off after that point. Sounds great, and IVAs were originally introduced as an alternative to the stigma of bankruptcy. Anyone who owes at least £15,000 to three or more creditors can arrange an IVA – but what is often forgotten is that an IVA is also a financial product being offered by agencies who take a healthy profit and thus have a vested interest in selling you that option.

IVAs are very attractive to those who feel swamped by debt because it means instant protection from creditors who no longer contact you, it provides protection from court action, and is not published in the local paper (unlike bankruptcy). Furthermore you can continue to have a current account (unlike bankruptcy), continue to trade as a business and you aren't disqualified from work in the financial sector. So what's not to like?

Well, for a start that IVA will typically stay on your credit record for six years (bankruptcy is just one) which may seem a small price to pay until you consider that your chances of getting business loans, overdrafts or a mortgage during that time are slim – to put it mildly. IVAs may be more discreet than bankruptcy but they typically last five times longer, are still recorded on a publicly searchable record and will be automatically converted to bankruptcy if you default. Do you really want to handcuff your potential to grow and raise money for that long in order to get out of a temporary scrape?

HERE'S AN IDEA FOR YOU...

Don't go to the private sector first for help getting out of a hole. Your interests are not necessarily the same as theirs. If you're in the UK, speak to the National Debtline (www.nationaldebtline.co.uk) instead or the charity Consumer Credit Counselling Service (www.cccs.co.uk) for free advice and debt management plans.

33 GET HELP

Money is complicated stuff and if you want to make the most of it you would do well to call in the experts. Or as Franklin said: *'they that won't be counseled, can't be helped.'*

DEFINING IDEA...

If you will not hear reason, she'll surely rap your knuckles.
~ BENJAMIN FRANKLIN

Paying out good money to someone else may not seem quite right on your individual way to wealth, but compared to doing the legwork yourself it is a quicker and more cost-effective way of getting the information you need to maximise your investments. That's presuming you pay out to the right people, of course.

Most of us make it through formal education blissfully untouched by any financial education other than the concept of happy hours in bars. Yet as adults we are suddenly bombarded with financial products that would have flummoxed Einstein.

Independent financial advisers (IFAs) offer unbiased advice on financial products either across the board or in a specialist field (such as mortgages). Choosing one at random out of the Yellow Pages is unlikely to produce the kind of person you get on with best, so the first step in selecting an adviser is to ask around – go to all of your more financially sorted friends for recommendations.

Try to narrow it down to two or three people and then ask for a 'getting to know' session with each one. This should be free – indeed, if it's not that may be an attitude you want to weigh up as part of deciding which one to plump for. Other things you should look for are the appropriate qualifications (in the UK, the starting point is all three components of the Financial Planning Certificate). Beyond that you should ask about any qualifications in the speciality you think is likely to be your main interest. Ask how long they've been in business and in what areas they have had their greatest successes.

Remember to ask about other clients. See if they can describe their typical client and consider whether you fit that bill – but do be realistic. Don't be tempted to bracket yourself with the millionaire Monaco playboys they work for if your own life is mainly spent in a two-bed semi-detached house in the suburbs of a provincial city. Ask whether their current clients would endorse them and take the number of one who would agree to be contacted. Check that the adviser is being regulated and by what body.

Your first session should also cover the question of whether payment will be by a fee or a commission. You should be given a choice in this matter and this is also the time to ask about how accessible the adviser is by phone and email, as well as in face-to-face meetings.

Don't forget the personality factor when you're choosing a financial adviser, either. Since you are going to be spending time discussing the details of your life with this individual, it must be someone who makes you feel both comfortable and reassured.

HERE'S AN IDEA FOR YOU...

For all the formal questions about qualifications and specialities, the big one you should lead with is 'what can you do for me?'. How well the IFA answers that, including precise figures of what money they expect to make and over what time, should probably be the decider for you.

34 DIY

For every corporate raider there are hundreds of Dilbert drones whiling away their days in the bowels of big business dreaming of better things. So get out there and work for yourself. As the man said: *'if you would have a faithful servant, and one that you like, serve yourself.'*

DEFINING IDEA…

Sexual harassment at work…
is it a problem for the self-employed?
~ VICTORIA WOOD, COMEDIAN AND WRITER

Working for yourself is something everyone has daydreamed about. Well, everyone with a boss, anyway. In our dreams it is the perfect way to wealth – a path uncluttered with office politics and the blinkers of others. As self-employed people, we picture ourselves as the ideal combination of worker and employer rolled into one, free at last to work how we like and achieve our goals.

The reality isn't always so sweet. Self-employment often means working much longer hours and with little or no guarantee of regular income. You're also going to have to sort out your own sick pay, pension, tax and probably VAT. Because if you don't then you have a rude awakening coming your way.

If you can possibly manage it, then the best way of setting yourself up in business is to start from a position of employment. All too often people try to start up on their own as a result of being made redundant or failing to get a job they applied for, and while a lot of these are successes it's not the easiest route. Instead test the waters before you make the leap and prepare for your new life financially and mentally.

Sort your finances out first. There are no businesses free from overheads and it pays to find out what your outgoings are and what can legitimately be claimed back from tax. Which brings us to point two – get an accountant if you haven't already. If you're thinking of trading as a limited company then you have no choice on the issue but even if you aim to be a sole trader you'll find that an accountant is a good idea because:

- They have an unbiased, unemotional view of your finances.

- They have more experience than you.

- They provide a first line of protection between you and the tax authorities.

- They, unlike you, won't be surprised when the tax bill arrives.

That last point is worth mentioning twice. You will be liable for tax, and just about everything else, so plan for it in advance and put aside money as you earn it. That takes real discipline, but if you don't then you will have palpitations when the taxman demands his cut.

Finally, do your research. Whether you're forming a co-operative, opening a franchise or setting up a partnership make sure that there is a market for what you have to offer. If you're already in employment in the same field then discreetly sort out your first clients – but be very careful not to put yourself in a position where your current employer can legitimately claim that you have stolen business from them.

HERE'S AN IDEA FOR YOU...

If you're in the UK and want to get a handle on your tax liability and what you can claim there is a helpline run by the Inland Revenue for the newly self employed. In the US try tax advice at Self Employed Web – www.selfemployedweb.com/last-minute-tax-filers.htm. An online search will bring up other relevant options.

35 BUILDING YOUR OWN BRAND

You are your own brand. The only difference between your brand and those of the big multinationals is that the only person marketing yourself is you, or as Benjamin put it, *'a man's own care is profitable'*.

Whether employed, self-employed or working on that big break as a beach bum, you are a brand with recognised values and selling points. People who are self-employed usually recognise that they are a brand; so do some others. For example, if you're a consultant or a knowledge worker you will already be familiar with the idea that your marketability is not simply the skill you offer but a whole suite of attributes including your social skills, appearance, associates, availability and pricing.

If you haven't thought of yourself in that way then you can start by asking yourself the following questions:

- What five words would other people use to describe me professionally?
- What are my best attributes as other people see them?
- Who is my target market? My boss? A new boss? My clients? New clients?
- What have I done in the last three months that has raised my profile with my target market?
- What do I plan on doing in the next three months that will raise my profile with my target market?

Don't confuse building a brand with doing your job. The work you do is a crucial part of the brand, but the brand goes well beyond what you deliver. For example, a lot of smart business people raise their visibility through activities such as volunteering, lecturing, working with mentors or being interviewed by analysts or journalists. Few of these things earn money directly and most don't fall under the heading of 'the day job', but they all build profile, recognition and what marketing people would dub 'brand equity'.

Think carefully about how to go above and beyond delivering on your job by being seen to excel and stand out. That doesn't necessarily mean doing the best job – those quiet, self-effacing workers who get everything done and take no credit themselves may get their reward in heaven but it's the self-marketers who reap the crops here on earth.

Consider how your current work project tallies with your perceived (or hoped for) branding. Does it challenge you? Does it highlight your best points? Will that come to the attention of those people you'd like to impress? If not, are you really sure that you are expending your efforts in the right direction? If you have the luxury of including self-branding as one of your criteria when taking on work, then that's great – but if you don't determine your own role so clearly, you can still use the idea to help decide where to really push for it and where to simply get by.

HERE'S AN IDEA FOR YOU...

Networking is key to brand development. Online networking sites like LinkedIn (www.linkedin.com) are obvious tools here but don't forget the power of Facebook (www.facebook.com). Time to remove that pic of you puking at the party and start marketing yourself more slickly.

36 THE KIND OF CREDIT THAT DOESN'T COME WITH APRS

Your chief job is marketing the brand that is you. But what if someone else is reaping the benefit of your branding efforts? *'Trusting too much to others' care is the ruin of many,'* as Franklin put it – and in this case trusting others to give you your due could be the ruin of your brand.

In the world of brands there is such a thing as 'ambush marketing' in which one brand relies on the equity built up by another, then steals its thunder. A classic example is the major sporting event where one shoe brand sponsors the whole shebang, only for its rival to park a truck right outside with a vast, unmissable LED screen showing its own adverts. In the business of me-branding the ambush comes when a colleague coolly claims credit for the fruits of your labour.

Since this is your brand at stake here, you can't take that sitting down – but nor do you want to appear too precious and whiny about the issue. Somehow you need to come out on top and smelling of roses, which can be tricky if the person claiming your credit happens to be your boss.

The first thing to consider is Franklin's own warning that trouble comes from trusting too much to the care of others. Undoubtedly praise from others carries more weight than blowing your own trumpet, but it is your job to ensure that you are getting noticed by other people. If someone else is getting credit you have to ask yourself whether you are being deliberately pushed out of praise's way or whether you have been too backward in coming forward.

Before you even think of mentioning your grievance consider the following:

- Has someone knowingly taken credit for your work
  or is it a misunderstanding?

- Has a manager simply taken credit for team leading or are
  they overstepping that line and specifically usurping your role?

If there is even the shadow of a doubt about the answer to either of these questions, then throwing your toys out of the pram at this stage is going to be counterproductive.

The best policy, certainly the first time it happens, is to give them the benefit of the doubt. If it happens again then put away your personal feelings of being wronged and instead see it as an opportunity to approach the purloiner of praise and express how happy you are to see that person drawing attention to the quality of your work. Maybe there's a way you can work together here… As with any negotiating position, the key is deciding what it is you want. Is it recognition, or are you prepared to put aside your branding issues with others, at this point, in return for the credit-taker's appreciation of what you do and the possibility that together you could go further?

HERE'S AN IDEA FOR YOU…

Plagiarising is a dangerous game with a double-edged blade, so if you are going to insinuate that it's happening, make sure you've already consulted with a third party beforehand about your position. This also gives you the benefit of an independent viewpoint about whether you are making an inappropriate fuss.

37 DON'T SELL YOURSELF SHORT – GET THAT RISE

Though a religious man, Franklin was clear that if you want to prosper you shouldn't be asking for divine help all the time. *'God helps them that help themselves,'* he insists, and oddly enough so do employers. If you don't take steps to get what you want then nobody else will do it for you.

Whilst there are many reasons why we seek employment (the challenge, the fulfilment, the kudos), and many things we appreciate (the environment, the social company, the free coffee), the heart of the employer/employee relationship is still the salary cheque. For all the challenge – and no matter how good the office banter and free drinks – there is little doubt that the size of that monthly figure is what makes most of us turn up on Monday mornings. So are you sure that you're being paid your worth? And what can you do about it if you're not?

Unless you're in a heavily-unionised or public-sector job with fixed pay levels the chances are that you and your colleagues remain firmly in the dark about each other's salaries – and the company is more than happy for it to stay that way.

To get an idea of what you should be paid you may have to look outside your own company. The first place to start is job adverts, but these can be misleading due to different packages of bonuses, compensation for stress or weighting for living in a more expensive part of the country.

Do your research carefully before walking into the boss's office – the fact that you know of another person in the company who earns more for the same job is not enough. Instead, see if you can point to a general industry standard of reward which you don't seem to be getting. Inflation is currently too low to be a major factor (though this may change), so unless you can bring absolute proof that fuel/food prices are hitting you more than others you must be prepared to show that you are underpaid for your market worth. Be aware that if you are a woman this is most likely the case anyway. Even so, prepare your argument – there is nothing worse than triumphantly pointing to a male co-worker who is earning more only to be told that they have a qualification or speciality known to your boss but not to you.

Finally, don't start questioning the level of your pay rise just when you've been told what it is, as a fait accompli is hard to overturn. Instead think about what you rightly deserve months before pay negotiations come around. The exception to that rule is if you feel you have just been personally key in a major coup for the company. Then it's time to strike while the iron is hot but – again – be sure to do your homework and not just make up a number.

HERE'S AN IDEA FOR YOU...

Instead of scouring the job adverts and sidling up to colleagues to ask their salaries, try an online salary checker. There are plenty of these for specific industries, roles and physical locations. One good example is www.worksmart.org.uk/tools/paywizard.php but they exist for pretty much any job and geographical area.

38 WORK SMARTER, NOT HARDER

Working smarter is another management maxim seen as a modern development, but the seed of the idea was there back in 1758 when Benjamin advised us to *'let us then be up and be doing, and doing to the purpose; so by diligence shall we do more with less perplexity'*.

An enthusiastic advocate of hard work, Franklin was not blind to the fact that labour for labour's sake is not in itself a virtue and that real productivity goes hand in hand with the ability to focus on the real goals and deliverables.

The working culture of long hours and lunchtimes snatched at the keyboard is no longer the purely Anglo-Saxon phenomenon it once was. Increasingly, employees feel they are expected to put in long hours in order to show commitment. Often this culture comes in by means of an insidious creep, where nobody wants to be seen to go home earliest or take the longest lunch break, and a lose/lose escalation kicks off.

Working smarter can really be boiled down to a combination of personal organisation, prioritising and (where appropriate) delegation – in that order.

Personal organisation starts with managing your diary at the very least, and project management software if that's what you are using. A lot of work crises that seem to ambush us at the last minute are, if we are honest with ourselves, entirely predictable were we to spend a little more time with our diaries working out deadline clashes. If your project is very complicated then project management software, with its ability to track and schedule multiple stages and tasks within a single project, is well worth the investment in both finance and learning that you need to get up to speed.

Prioritisation goes hand in hand with organisation. You have to be absolutely ruthless about which deadlines are critical and which are merely desirable. It's a classic human error to waste time dabbling on two projects rather than focusing on just one, or to be distracted into working on the more attractive one despite it being less urgent.

Delegating is part of prioritising. If you've managed your time looking forwards and realise that you're not going to be able to satisfy the demands on you, then you may need to look to some personal outsourcing if you're still going to hit your goals. Small businesses, sole traders and self-made entrepreneurs are notoriously bad at this since they tend to resent paying anyone else for something they can do themselves. Often, however, this means that while your clients pay you for a skill they value, you are wasting your own time on skills they don't – such as bookkeeping or admin. We know it's not cost effective, but many of us spend hours doing petty tasks that could easily be batched up and handed off to someone else for a fraction of the hourly rate we ourselves are worth.

HERE'S AN IDEA FOR YOU...

Working to a tight deadline? Stop multitasking. Close down your email and switch your phone to voicemail. Research suggests that we only manage three continuous minutes of work before being interrupted. Taking intrusive but impersonal interruptions out of the equation makes you much more likely to get your work done.

39 BEWARE OF BARGAINS

Like Pavlov's dogs we can't help but salivate at the sound of the word 'bargain'. And yet as Franklin points out '… *many have been ruined by buying good pennyworths'.* **With a looming financial slowdown that has never been truer.**

Somehow a bargain is more than a financial saving; it encompasses a sense of opportunity not to be lost and even a degree of wisdom in the choice. There is a Monty Python sketch featuring the British comedians dressed up as housewives discussing their day:

Mrs Non-Gorilla: 'Have you been shopping?'

Mrs Gorilla: 'No … been shopping.'

Mrs Non-Gorilla: 'Did you buy anything?'

Mrs Gorilla: 'A piston engine!' She reveals a six-cylinder car engine on a white tray, on a trolley.

Mrs Non-Gorilla: 'What d'you buy that for?'

Mrs Gorilla: 'Oooh! It was a bargain.'

While he was unlikely to have had piston engines in mind, Franklin's 'good pennyworths' are exactly the same idea – items with prices that tempt us to snap them up without due consideration of their real value. *'And again, at a great pennyworth pause a while: he means, that perhaps the cheapness is apparent only, and not real; or the bargain, by straitning thee in thy business, may do thee more harm than good.'*

Of course any bargain is only a bargain if it is a price cut on an item you needed to buy anyway. A bargain that leads you into buying goods or services you were otherwise happy without isn't a bargain at all – it's a loss, and any theoretical saving is not only a waste of money but, more crucially, a waste of cash.

With a credit crunch already biting and a potential recession in the offing, a bargain ceases to be a bargain if it damages your cash flow. To genuinely evaluate a bargain for your business you can't just take into account the price; you must also consider the terms of payment. Hard as it may be to turn down, any bargain that puts a strain on cash reserves is probably not a saving you can afford. Maintaining positive cash flow can be more important than generating profit or scoring that 'bargain', since a lack of ready cash brings with it the risk of failing to meet liabilities – with the likely result of insolvency. If that happens, the receiver will investigate your behaviour and if it turns out that you failed to meet payments to creditors due to a hoped-for long-term saving, that bargain could cost you dear.

The flip side of this is that you can make your own offerings into a 'bargain' that encourages positive cash flow. Whether you deal in products or services, you can improve your cash flow by giving discounts in return for prompt payment or insisting on deposits in advance for jobs that you are taking on.

HERE'S AN IDEA FOR YOU...

Tempted by a bargain? Don't pay for it now. Instead make sure you're making the most of payment terms. If payment can be agreed on in, say, thirty days, don't pay before then and make sure you use a prompt payment system, such as electronic transfer, to ensure you pay on time.

40 LOOK BEYOND THE PURCHASE PRICE

The price tag is often only the beginning of the payment. If you or your business buy anything then consider the ongoing maintenance costs, not just the purchase price. Or as Franklin put it: '... 'tis easier to build two chimneys than to keep one in fuel'.

They think they can make fuel from horse manure – now, I don't know if your car will be able to get thirty miles to the gallon, but it's sure gonna put a stop to siphoning.

~ BILLIE HOLIDAY

Fuel is as timely a topic as ever, albeit one more associated with cars than chimneys. When buying cars we realise that there will be ongoing costs in the form of petrol, but we rarely take into account the full impact of standing charges and running costs. Standing charges are the costs you pay whether or not you use the vehicle. That means tax, insurance, the cost of the capital used (on a purchase plan), depreciation and breakdown cover. Running costs are mainly fuel but also all those little things you're busy tucking to the back of your mind – parking, servicing, repairs, wear and tear, etc.

In the UK the AA (Automobile Association) provides tables to help you calculate the cost of running and standing costs depending on the cost of your vehicle. You may be horrified to learn that with a car worth £10,000, driven around 20,000 miles a year, the combined running and standing costs come to about 30p per mile. So that's £6000 per year. More than you thought? Undoubtedly, and that figure was based on fuel prices that have since risen dramatically. Buy yourself a more expensive car and the cost per annum soars, not just because it uses more fuel but because of the factor depreciation plays in the costs.

Depreciation, the AA informs us, is 'the biggest cost after fuel purchase' and yet the chances are that it's the factor least likely to be considered when buying personal or company transport. Partly that's because it's not an exact science, with different models depreciating less based not just on their perceived build quality but also on their popularity – a factor which varies. It may come as a surprise to find that a typical new car will lose 40% of its value in the first year just because it is no longer new, but if it is a model in particular demand that figure can be reduced to as little as 10%.

The first year is the biggest bite out of the value of the car just because it no longer boasts that 'fresh from the showroom' appeal but by the end of year three a typical car will have lost 60% of its value. Compare that with the cost of capital if you are buying on a credit scheme and you can see that the initial purchase price is really only the tip of the iceberg. Which is why the most cost-effective car is probably a five-year-old model with a low mileage…

HERE'S AN IDEA FOR YOU…

Most of us use cars for work or personal reasons but do you need to own those wheels? Leasing provides a means of managing depreciation and helps plan ahead by setting a fixed monthly cost (usually including servicing). If you're doing major mileage it can also prove the cheapest option.

41 CUSTOMER RETENTION

Franklin was a great believer in putting down roots in business. When he says *'I never saw an oft removed tree, nor yet an oft removed family, that throve so well as those that settled be'*, he was clearly referring to the joys of being established.

Nowadays location is not so critical to business, but other forms of establishment certainly are.

While just about every business pays lip service to the importance of customer retention and creating a community around a brand, product or service, the fact is that the vast majority remain far more interested in customer acquisition. So much so that a survey by Accenture a couple of years ago found that boardrooms in the UK ranked maximising revenue from existing customers at the bottom of their list of objectives. Franklin could have told them, however, that as natural as that may be, it is also wrong.

Email, mobile phones and online shopping have all helped erode the amount of contact between businesses and their customers, but that only means that each touch point is all the more important. At a time when it has never been easier to take your custom elsewhere customer retention is crucial, but many companies don't even have effective mechanisms for monitoring customer attrition, let alone for doing anything about it.

The first step is to start to measure attrition, meaning the number of your clients who don't go on to repeat their purchase or renew their relationship with you. That should be done over an appropriate trading period and expressed as a percentage of the total. The next step is to go back to the old 80:20 rule and see if it applies to your business. Typically some 80% of a business's profits come from just 20% of the customers – time to start expending more effort on targeting that 20% and ensuring you deliver the service they expect. This demands a CRM (Customer Relation Management) system. If you are a one-man band with only a few clients then your CRM could be as simple as good people skills, nice manners and a razor-sharp memory. For pretty much everybody else, however, it's worth investing in CRM software.

Software alone won't do it, though. To keep customers happy you need staff who share your ideals and are sufficiently empowered and motivated to deliver them. Complaints shouldn't be swept under the carpet; they should be reported – and acted on.

Nor is fixing a complaint the end of the process. It should be followed by a review of the lessons and communication to other customers to let them know that you're on the case. Make sure that everyone, no matter how senior, gets to experience just what it is like to be one of your customers, and one of the staff that deals with them. It's because boardrooms become so distant from the customer that they lose sight of the importance of keeping their existing clientèle.

HERE'S AN IDEA FOR YOU...

You don't have to be a supermarket or an airline to introduce a loyalty scheme. They can be scaled to suit the size of your enterprise and could be as simple as theatre tickets or a bottle of wine sent to anyone who makes a repeat order or spends a certain amount.

42 DON'T GET TOO COCKY

There's a fine line between confidence and arrogance in business. Or, as Franklin put it, *'Great estates may venture more, But little boats should keep near shore.'*

Confidence often provides the 'get up and go' that is essential to success, but if it tips over into arrogance it is likely to lead to bad judgement, taking on more than you are truly capable of and overestimating your abilities.

DEFINING IDEA...

Action and reaction, ebb and flow, trial and error, change – this is the rhythm of living. Out of our overconfidence, fear; out of our fear, clearer vision, fresh hope. And out of hope, progress.

~ BRUCE BARTON, AMERICAN AUTHOR, ADVERTISING EXECUTIVE AND POLITICIAN

A recent study by the University of Leicester and the Economic and Social Research Council found that those business people most confident of their ability were also the most likely to fail. Dr. Pulford, from the University's School of Psychology, said, 'When success depended on skill, overconfidence tended to cause excess entry into a marketplace

… market-entry decisions tend to be over-optimistic, with the inevitable result that new business start-ups tend to exceed market capacity, and many new businesses fail within a few years.'

The commonest reason for this was that the overconfidence led them to leap into new ventures without sufficient research or respect for the opposition and the hurdles to be overcome. In particular, they overestimated the capacity of a market to support a new player, and the attraction that their novelty would have for existing customers.

Overconfidence is more common than you think. Consider these figures from investment advisors The Motley Fool:

- 82% of people say they are in the top 30% of safe drivers.

- 86% of Harvard Business School students say they are better looking than their classmates.

- 81% of new business owners think their business has at least a 70% chance of success, but only 39% think any business like theirs would be likely to succeed.

So what can we do to 'keep near shore'?

The first step is to honestly admit our own limitations. That means being realistic about what we really think we can do and not confusing it with what we dream of being able to do.

The second one is to remember that we are always learning and we simply never know enough. There is no substitute for good research and the tools for researching a market have never been better or more easily available – but all the tools in the world are of no avail if we don't bother to use them.

The third step is to beware of presumptions. Never presume that competitors are wrong simply because they don't have your forward-thinking attitude. It's tempting to dismiss the established opposition as being slow-moving, entrenched dinosaurs and, who knows, maybe they are. But if you allow yourself to work on that assumption without examining the reasons for their behaviour you may be missing a major hurdle to market entry.

HERE'S AN IDEA FOR YOU...

Picture your own company from an outsider's point of view, and try to be objective about the likelihood of its success. You will need help, so ask an unbiased third party about the chances and the risks. Now for the tricky bit – listen to them.

43 PREPARE FOR THE WORST

We're often so busy getting on with business that we don't really have time to learn from our mistakes but, as Franklin would have been the first to point out, learning is what distinguishes the smart from the stupid: *'wise men learn by others' harms, fools scarcely by their own'*.

DEFINING IDEA...

I always tried to turn every disaster into an opportunity.

~ JOHN D. ROCKEFELLER

Nobody wants to dwell on the possible downsides of commerce because if we focused on everything that could go wrong we'd probably never get out of bed in the morning, never mind get into business. Totally ignoring the potential pitfalls, however, is nearly as bad as cockiness and overconfidence. According to UK bank Lloyds TSB, nearly half of all small businesses fail within their first three years, and while one in five businesses suffers some kind of major disruption in a year a crushing 80% of small and medium enterprises (SMEs) fail to recover if it happens to them and close down within the next eighteen months.

The vast majority of smaller enterprises have no emergency plan to cope with major troubles such as flooding, fire, vandalism or terrorism and yet it is precisely the SMEs that have the least resources in reserve to keep them afloat if they are forced to stop trading for any period of time. Be absolutely honest; have you drawn up your worst-case scenario? And if you have, do you have a plan for dealing with it other than curling into a small ball and hiding under your desk?

If you came up short on the above question then it's time to follow Franklin and look around at 'others' harms'. Trade publications are a pretty good starting point since there isn't an industry newspaper in print that doesn't lead with the cock-ups of your peers. Missing deadlines, penalty clauses, power cuts, industrial accidents, mass layoffs – they are the stock in trade of your industry press and while it certainly isn't cheerful reading, it is a mine of information on the things that can go wrong. Instead of the schadenfreude of watching your opposition struggle in terrible circumstances, consider carefully how badly your own enterprise would be hit if it faced a similar or worse scenario.

Think carefully about the following:

- Are you insured for damage to your stock, your premises and your possessions if disaster strikes?

- Are you protected in the event of loss of earnings so that your bills will continue to be paid even if you or your business have to cease or restrict trading?

- Do you have a fallback plan and an emergency fund to keep the business ticking over until you can get back to full speed?

Insurance is a great thing, but don't get too smug just because you're insured. The real mark of preparation is not being compensated for the disaster a year after your company closes; it's keeping your company's head above the flood waters until everything is back to normal.

HERE'S AN IDEA FOR YOU...

Don't forget your data. Would you survive without order books, customer contact details and intellectual property? No, so don't just back them up locally to tape or CD – a hosting company can provide you with a mirror copy of all crucial data hosted on a remote server away from your premises.

44 MAKE FRIENDS WITH A MENTOR

Franklin thought the principle of learning from other people's mistakes was such a good idea he opted to say it all over again – in Latin. *'Felix quem faciunt aliena pericula cautum'*, he intoned which, if your Latin is a little rusty, roughly translates as 'happy is he who learns caution from the perils of other people'.

Worst-case scenarios are helpful but there's a less painful way of learning from others than drawing them up. Franklin's point that 'wise men learn by others' harms' is the thinking behind the whole process of mentoring which is rapidly gaining popularity as an alternative to traditional consultancy.

DEFINING IDEA...

Learn from the mistakes of others. You can't live long enough to make them all yourself.
~ ELEANOR ROOSEVELT

If you're running an SME then a business mentor provides a number of roles. They are a sounding board for your ideas and a trusted third party ready with unbiased opinions about the wisdom of your plans.

They also go a long way to easing the loneliness that goes with shouldering an SME on your own. After all, who else can you freely turn to? Of course you have a bank manager, friends and family but, unlike all of them, a mentor really does want to talk about your business and is happy to spare whatever time that takes.

But most of all they've been there, done that and got the T-shirt. Which means they bring with them all of the mistakes they themselves made and the answers to those mistakes, without you having to go through that painful process yourself. A mentor also brings with them all the networking contacts they have made during the course of their own entrepreneurial activities which can prove an invaluable short cut for the SME in a hurry.

Typically a mentor is someone who has 'made it', in whatever terms they define 'it', and now has the time to give something back. If they're any good, they are also in the learning business themselves and aim to pick up as much from you as you will from them. Which brings me to the last and most wonderful thing about a mentor – mentoring is usually free since the quid pro quo is the learning exchange. If you're running an SME then good, free advice is not something you can afford to pass up on.

It's not difficult to find a mentor and while there are paid-for services available online there are also a lot of programmes being offered by the governments of the UK (try local government and organisations like The Prince's Trust), Canada, NZ, and the US (try the Small Business Development Centers). Remember that with a mentor the more you put into it the more you both get out of it, so try to meet up as much as possible. That in turn means it's best if you get on well enough to spend serious time in each other's company – so choose wisely.

HERE'S AN IDEA FOR YOU...

Start by 'auditioning' a number of possible mentors. Begin by brainstorming your goals for the relationship, then arrange to meet a select few for a 'one off' meeting to find who you click best with. See which person has the most input on your brainstormed list and take it from there.

45 GO FOR IT

Franklin was keenly aware of the dangers of overconfidence or brashness, but don't confuse that with lack of commitment. Pussyfooting around was no more desirable in Franklin's day than it is now or, as he put it, *'handle your tools without mittens; remember that the cat in gloves catches no mice.'*

DEFINING IDEA...

Success or failure in business is caused more by mental attitude than by mental capacities.
~ SIR WALTER SCOTT

Even if the phrasing sounds somewhat old-fashioned, the thinking is bang up to date. Entrepreneurship isn't a business model but an attitude, and one that thrives on getting down and dirty with the nuts and bolts of the business which you have made your own. You will need deep reserves of commitment, self-confidence (not to be confused with arrogance, do note), persistence and the initiative to be a true self-starter.

Before taking the plunge into your own business venture try the Attitude Check List:

- You believe that failure is not an option.

- The goals of this enterprise are 100% yours.

- You have crystal-clear objectives.

- You are ready to step up to the plate and ask that others around you do the same.

- You recognise that there are risks but are excited by the challenge.

- Quitting is not an option.

- You know exactly what you need to do to take this business to the next level.

- You know exactly what it will take to deliver on your promises.

- You inspire those you work with.

- You're not afraid to make commitments around the business.

Can you tick off ten out of ten on that list? If not, it doesn't mean that you shouldn't be taking the plunge but it does mean there's an area that you are not completely convinced about. If that's the case then you need to address it now. Commitment to succeeding is a crucial part of the formula and, odd though it sounds, people are often as afraid of success as they are of failure. If you answered yes to the above questions but are still hesitating, then ask yourself if you are more nervous about the risks of success than failure. A lot of us hold back because it's easier to coast along than to admit that this time we are going for gold.

The other point to remember is that unless you are going solo, you'll have co-workers or employees, and for you to succeed they have to be every bit as motivated. You should be an inspiration to everyone you work with but being a role model is only a part of that strategy – you will also need to think yourself into their shoes, understand their tasks and motivate them to share the same drive. Pussyfooting around is not an option with other people any more than it is with yourself. If you are in any way uncertain when discussing your mutual goals with your co-workers, then you are creating potential danger areas for misunderstandings later.

HERE'S AN IDEA FOR YOU...

Getting hands on doesn't have to mean micromanaging. Really knowing the nuts and bolts of a business can make you a more inspiring leader and give you the edge in negotiating with your staff, so don't distance yourself from the engine room – roll up your sleeves and get stuck in.

46 MANAGING OTHERS

The way to wealth is rarely a solitary path and how well you work with your fellow travellers is going to be a large part of whether you succeed or fail. Failure to manage those who work for you is an expensive business – or as Franklin would have it *'not to oversee workmen is to leave them your purse open'.*

Back in Franklin's day the idea of overseeing probably had a more literal sense of keeping an eye on workmen to ensure that they didn't slack off and that they did do the task as required.

In order that people may be happy in their work, these three things are needed: They must be fit for it. They must not do too much of it. And they must have a sense of success in it.
~ JOHN RUSKIN

For the modern manager, the risks of slacking off or open dishonesty, while still there, are probably lower than the far more common and insidious risk of teams failing to perform to their potential due to inadequate coaching. Overseeing in the modern environment isn't about making staff nervous by watching them like a hawk, it's about being a quality team leader. For that there are a number of rules to bear in mind.

- The first step in super-supervision is being absolutely clear about what the goal of the project is and what must be done on the way.

- The second is to ensure that your staff fully understand that. It's very easy to overlook the fact that just because someone is good at what they do, doesn't mean they know what they're doing on this job. And, conversely, just because someone doesn't know what they're doing on this project doesn't mean they're not good at what they do.

- Don't just consider the short-term goals – discuss the ultimate outcomes so that those working for you can see your expectations and your point of view. If you share the same understanding of the ultimate outcome, rather than just a job description of the task at hand, you are more likely to arrive at the same goal.

- Make sure you are asking the right people to do the job and make your needs and expectations as clear as possible. Get people to explain back to you what needs to be done and how it has to happen to ensure they've really got it.

- Make sure deadlines are also perfectly clear and understood by all, and don't wait until the end of a task to review it. Build in some kind of review along the way to catch problems before they develop into full-blown crises.

- If things do go wrong, remember the old rule of praising in public but criticising in private.

Finally, make a point of awarding rewards that are appropriate to the goals. That could be a simple matter of fixing a price or it could entail bonuses for overachieving – but any member of staff will be more motivated by appropriate, goal-based rewards tied to a job of work.

HERE'S AN IDEA FOR YOU...

Catch people doing things right. Inexperienced supervisors believe they are there to act like prison guards watching out for misbehaviour, but you will get much better results by turning that on its head and pouncing in order to praise good work when you see it.

47 THINK AHEAD

Although Franklin doesn't mention pensions per se, he would definitely have approved. He even appears to pave the way to pensions when he says *'At present, perhaps, you may think yourself in thriving circumstances, and that you can bear a little extravagance without injury; but, for age and want, save while you may'.*

DEFINING IDEA...

Always be nice to bankers. Always be nice to pension fund managers. Always be nice to the media. In that order.

~ JOHN GOTTI, US GANGSTER

'He that lives upon hope will die fasting,' Franklin adds, which is a slightly grim but possibly accurate summation of our position if we don't plan for old age. There's something uncool about talking pensions, particularly amongst the young, but there again there's something much more uncool about living off tinned food in a small flat when you could be sipping cocktails by the beach.

If you're counting on a state pension to take care of you in your golden years then that gold is going to lose its shine pretty fast. Simply put, more of us are living longer (particularly women) and since the workforce isn't growing that means fewer active workers putting money into the pot to pay for those claiming retirement benefits. It's not quite as simple as that since workers are more productive these days, earnings continue to rise, and there's the less cheerful factor that growing obesity means the next generation may halt or even reverse the trend of longer life. Despite that, the essential picture is that anyone counting solely on a state pension is likely to be leading a much less rewarding retired life than those who start to save with a private pension or investment plan.

There are hundreds of different pension plans out there but essentially three major approaches (if we ignore the basic state pension). The first is to contribute to your employer's pension scheme. This is probably the most cost-effective, since the normal arrangement is that your employer either tops up your contribution or may match it – so you end up with more than you paid in. These days there is, however, a certain cynicism about company pensions due to unscrupulous executives raiding them. Such cases are rare but if you are genuinely hesitant about trusting your future to your company then consider a personal pension scheme.

Private pensions are still better than most other savings because most governments give them sizeable tax breaks and some even help top up your contributions. Again there have been scandals with banks failing and pension schemes evaporating, but these are extremely rare and where investment companies are covered by national banking codes individual investors should get their money back.

The third main approach is to go for investments such as property. This can be personally satisfying and a great deal more fun than simply paying into a pension fund managed by another, but you are unlikely to benefit from the same kind of tax benefits extended to more formal schemes. Don't forget to consider the risks, though.

HERE'S AN IDEA FOR YOU...

Don't think about a pension, think about lots of pensions. Diversify and spread your risk across a mix of tax-free savings, investments and formal pension schemes. For example, rather than buying a property think about investing in a property fund and spreading your investment that way.

48 DON'T FALL BEHIND YOUR BUSINESS

Ever had the feeling you're running flat out to keep up with your business? While he tied the concept to the notion of getting up early (a key belief), Franklin also observed that some of us seem to spend all day chasing our own shadows: *'he that riseth late, must trot all day, and shall scarce overtake his business at night'*.

There are, of course, two responses. The first is not to get up late and thereby give yourself an early start. That's sound advice now as ever, but with business life and time demands getting ever more complex you may feel that you are still running just to end up in one place.

People who create 20% of the results will begin believing they deserve 80% of the rewards.
~ PAT RILEY, FORMER NBA HEAD COACH, WITH HIS TAKE ON THE PARETO PRINCIPLE.

Which means it's time to turn to triage. The word 'triage' comes from the French for sorting or ordering things and is most famously used by battlefield medics selecting which patients to give their attention to, and in which order, so as to maximise the benefits of their limited resources. A similar principle can be brought to bear on your priorities during the day. Not that I'm saying your business day looks like the bloody carnage of a battlefield, just that it can seem that way…

In the 1940s the quality management pioneer Dr Juran came up with the theory of 'the vital few and trivial many' and named it after an Italian economist called Vilfredo Pareto who had observed that in his home country

80% of the wealth was in the hands of just 20% of the population. Hence the Pareto Principle, whereby 20% of something (the vital few) is always responsible for 80% of the results, and the remaining 80% (the trivial many) only accounts for 20% of the results. Confused? Don't be. In daily life the application of the Pareto principle means that, for example, 20% of the job (typically the first and last 10%) will take up 80% of the time and resources. Likewise a minority of 20% of your staff will do 80% of the work, and 20% of your staff will require 80% of your time managing them (rarely the same 20%, as it happens). The trick is to focus solely on the 20% that really counts and thereby achieve 80% of the work.

Wherever possible you should work with hard figures. Whether it's profit/loss, costs, time or headcount you can then draw up a 'Pareto' chart of the resource in question and find which part of the picture is the one to throw your energies at first. A simple Pareto analysis would list all the known problems associated with a project and count which ones occur most over a set time. Order them with the most frequent at the top and you may find that seemingly trivial problems add up to a huge cumulative loss of productivity. There's your starting point.

HERE'S AN IDEA FOR YOU...

Don't have any figures to tell you which 20% to focus on? Write a ten-point to-do list of things you have to do. Now rank that list one to ten in terms of importance, where one is least and ten is tops. Now forget about points one to eight until nine and ten are done.

49 BE READY TO LISTEN

Businesses spend a great deal of money on consultancy but that doesn't mean they act on the advice they're given. Franklin could have been speaking for every consultant out there when he said *'We may give advice, but we cannot give conduct'.*

In *The Secrets of Consulting* Gerald Weinberg established what he called the first and second laws of consulting. The first is that clients are not rational and although they have a problem (otherwise the consultant would not be there) they will never admit it. The second is that no matter how technical the problem may appear at first glance, it will ultimately prove to be a people problem.

Be honest, doesn't that sound just a little bit familiar? Nobody likes to admit to problems, essentially human ones, so even good advice is painful to act on. In particular, there's one refusal to act on advice that is so widespread it has its own name; founderitis, or Founder's Syndrome – the negative symptoms which can arise when a company founder has difficulty letting go and allowing the business to grow beyond his or her original dream.

The classic symptoms of founderitis include disrespect for new practices or formalised planning (the stock in trade of consultants), a disinclination to delegate and, above all, a resistance to advice from specialists. It's an understandable side-effect of the amount of personal investment it takes to get a new enterprise off the ground – the business becomes your baby and you are reluctant to give it up or to be told by someone else that they are better qualified to care for it. Except that, again like kids, businesses have a tendency to grow up and they change and evolve as they do so.

It's easy to grow by hiring people who specialise in areas you don't deal with, and relatively easy to take their advice and even defer to it. Sooner or later, however, you're going to have to hire people whose speciality overlaps with your home turf, either as consultants or staff, and at that point you will be forced to listen to advice that you have little inclination to respect more than your own. Why will you inevitably have to do that? Because even if you are very good at your key area, the fact that you guard it jealously means that you run the risk of becoming a bottleneck as every decision on that subject has to pass through you.

The only answer is to learn to step back and force yourself to ask for input from other people. Evaluate it, bring in third parties where appropriate to discuss it and then, finally, bite the bullet and act on it. If you don't think anyone has better advice to offer than you do, then either you should look to recruit staff you respect more, or you should be asking yourself seriously if you are in denial about being chronically stricken with founderitis yourself. Time to get real.

HERE'S AN IDEA FOR YOU...

Take a break. A real one; a holiday with no email, no voicemail and no calls to or from the office. Then come back two weeks later and open your eyes to the fact that the business is still going. Accept that and you are more likely to accept advice as a result.

50 BE CAREFUL OUT THERE

A firm opponent of dogma, Franklin nonetheless firmly believed that faith in (a) God should accompany every aspect of life. It is telling, therefore, that in *The Way to Wealth* he specifically says that *'In the affairs of this world men are saved not by faith, but by the want of it'*.

An extraordinarily capable man, Franklin (inventor, physicist, musician, writer, politician) clearly believed that we are responsible for our own endeavours and encouraged those around him to organise themselves to make their lives better. That's as clear from his actions as from his words, since he is seen as the founding father of both the first fire-fighting organisation and the first hospital in the US.

By urging us to rely on a lack of faith he is highlighting the risks involved in trusting your health and wealth to heaven, fate or blind optimism. It's a risk that particularly affects entrepreneurs who tend to be notably dynamic and (over)optimistic. In your excitement about your own business and wealth creation, then, you can be saved by not trusting to fate. Here are some things I bet you haven't taken into account…

Death and disability

Death marks the end of your own personal way to wealth, but if you're the principal breadwinner have you got life insurance in place for your dependants? Even if you have, the chances are that you haven't invested in disability insurance because a) you're too busy trying to make money to spend it on insurance, and b) you just don't want to think about it. Do consider it. You don't have to work with industrial machinery or have a risky occupation to wind up disabled; a stroke or heart attack will do just as good a job of incapacitating you.

Irreplaceable others

If you've chosen co-workers and employees carefully then you should have at least one you see as being invaluable. Which is great while their qualities are working on your behalf, but what if they leave? What happens to your business if a key employee has to move on? Do you have clients who are entirely dependent on a single relationship with one person? How much business would you lose if that individual went to a rival company? Entrepreneurs tend to live their business and often forget that it is far less all-consuming, satisfying or attractive for their staff than it is for them.

Globalisation and rivals

You've got a great idea and a great team to put it in place, so what can possibly go wrong? How about a rival in Taiwan coming up with the same thing using cheaper labour and selling their product directly into your market via the web? Don't trust that your brilliance will keep you ahead of the game or that this year's good idea will last for ever. Someone, somewhere will build a better mouse trap.

HERE'S AN IDEA FOR YOU...

Got an employee worth their weight in gold? Appoint them as a mentor to someone else and have that person shadow your wunderkind. In particular have them work as a team with clients so the shadow becomes seen as the apprentice and heir apparent to the star.

51 DON'T STOP BECAUSE YOU MAKE IT

The Way to Wealth isn't just about pointing yourself in the right direction; it's about keeping up the momentum on the way. Or as Franklin puts it: *'He that hath a calling hath an office of profit and honor; but then the trade must be worked at, and the calling well followed, or neither the estate, nor the office, will enable us to pay our taxes.'*

DEFINING IDEA...

It's never enough until your heart stops beating. The deeper you get, the sweeter the pain. Don't give up the game until your heart stops beating.

~ SHELLSHOCK, BY NEW ORDER

I once had a conversation with a venture capitalist about entrepreneurs in the UK. He explained that essentially they had two waves of entrepreneurs – the driving young types determined to prove themselves and make their mark, and then the second-time-around types. The latter were older men and women who had already 'made it', become millionaires and drifted into semi-retirement, only to find that they were bored and looking for a challenge.

Franklin's advice was set against a backdrop of less general affluence than today, and his point was that you must continue to work on your skills and abilities if you want to get the most out of your work life as well as pay your bills. What he didn't stress for his audience in the 1750s is that this advice holds true for those who have achieved success, as well as for those still struggling to find it.

You might think that you work your way to wealth because you want to achieve a certain level of comfort, kudos or satisfaction. What you will find is that once there you will (indeed, should want to) set new goals to continue your personal momentum. Otherwise you stagnate.

Goal setting is the key for this. Breaking down major tasks into more manageable goals is important, yes. What is equally important for your personal and business momentum, however, is to ensure there is always another, bigger goal out there on the horizon. Keeping a list of your goals is a great help, since looking back on what you aspired to two years ago helps you focus on what you have achieved since then and on what remains to be done. Setting goals without recognising your achievements en route can turn the way to wealth into a treadmill.

Don't fall into the rut of thinking that new goals simply means more of the old goals. Try to think laterally about what you might achieve differently. Don't be bashful about thinking big and putting your wildest dreams onto your list. If you are stuck for ideas about how wild your dreams should be, then try brainstorming with co-workers and friends about just how high you could all go. It doesn't matter that the wild dream is too big a goal to go for right now, just that it's in the picture and you're keeping that dream alive. You can work out steps to break down the dream into more easily digested chunks as you go.

HERE'S AN IDEA FOR YOU...

Mentoring is an excellent way of maintaining momentum because it freshens up your ideas with someone else's fresh start, makes you think about new problems in new ways, and increases your networking reach. Think about signing up as a mentor yourself.

52 BE REALISTIC

The very last message of *The Way to Wealth* is a very human one, namely that Franklin knows full well what people are like and how much notice they tend to take of good advice about thrift and hard work. After his 'harangue' is done he notes that *'The people heard it, and approved the doctrine, and immediately practiced the contrary'.*

We are all like the crowd in *The Way to Wealth* – we hear plenty of good advice, nod our approval and promptly ignore it. We know it doesn't make sense to have large credit card balances but we still use them as stop-gap loans. We are fully aware we buy things we don't strictly need, but the new i-Thingy is sooo bright, sooo shiny. Whatever advice Franklin gives us we will still be suckers for bargains, and we will still be tempted to keep up with our peers. As sure as tomorrow follows today, we will put off unpleasant jobs and will inevitably splash out on luxuries to reward or compensate ourselves for making it through the daily grind.

Franklin recognises that; in fact, his final point is that while the audience completely ignores the advice the one person struck by it, almost shamed by it indeed, is himself. *'I resolved to be the better for the echo of it',* he promises, *'and though I had at first determined to buy stuff for a new coat, I went away resolved to wear my old one a little longer.'* Having heard his own advice spoken back to him, he has at least decided to make one little concession and keep his old item of clothing for a while longer rather than replace it right then. It is a small step but, as he notes repeatedly throughout the treatise, such small steps add up to great savings if repeated and multiplied.

His final promise to us can therefore be seen as being at the same time very modest and very hopeful: *'reader, if thou wilt do the same, thy profit will be as great as mine,'* he says, knowing that the 'profit' in question is a short-term saving on a new coat, and an attitude that will stand you in good stead for life.

So don't go away thinking that Franklin's wisdom is all very well but barely workable. He himself concedes that while ideally you should go to bed early, work harder than everyone else, borrow nothing and purchase nothing but necessities, life isn't so straightforward. Instead if you take just one little tip from his ideas and apply it to your life that will be precisely the kind of small step that leads towards wealth. Or, to put it another way: one good idea can change your life.

HERE'S AN IDEA FOR YOU...

If you don't have time to put in practice all the ideas and themes of The Way to Wealth *then go to Idea 8,* To Thine Own Self be True *(p. 17), and begin by working out your finances. If you did that and nothing else you would be on the path to prosperity.*

INDEX